IMAGES
of America

CATONSVILLE

You always wanted
to live in Catonsville — well
you made it and then some.
Here's to dreaming.

Love,
Janie
2009

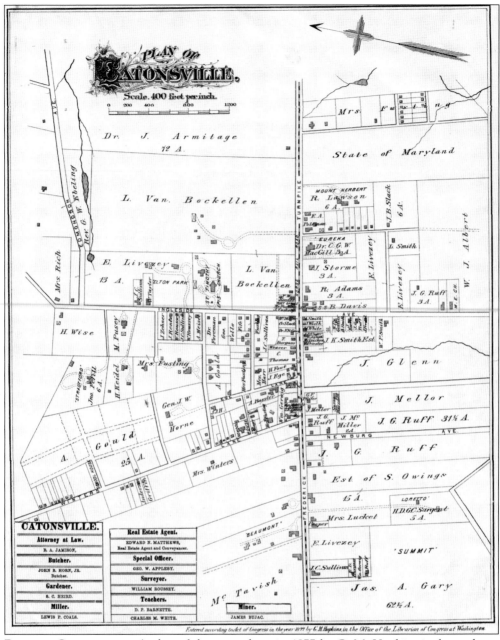

PLAN OF CATONSVILLE. A plan of the town done in 1877 by G. M. Hopkins is shown here. (Courtesy of Pam Kinzel.)

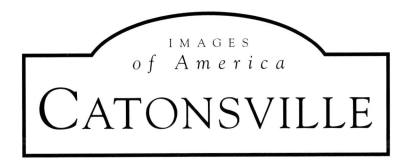

IMAGES
of America

CATONSVILLE

Marsha Wight Wise

ARCADIA
PUBLISHING

Published by Arcadia Publishing
Charleston SC, Chicago IL, Portsmouth NH, San Francisco CA

Printed in the United States of America

Library of Congress Catalog Card Number: 2005923384

For all general information contact Arcadia Publishing at:
Telephone 843-853-2070
Fax 843-853-0044
E-mail sales@arcadiapublishing.com
For customer service and orders:
Toll-Free 1-888-313-2665

Visit us on the Internet at www.arcadiapublishing.com

To the men in my life, John, Matthew, Jared, and Jason: you will always be my greatest achievements.

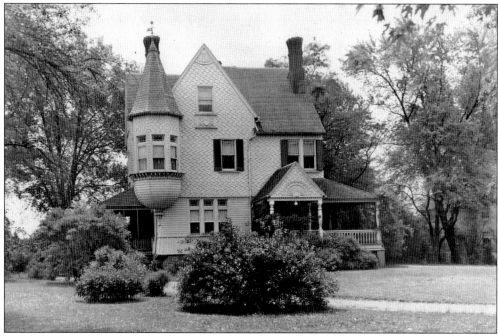

RESIDENCE OF G. B. JOBSON. This home is a wonderful example of the Queen Anne Victorian architecture that can still be found throughout Catonsville. The home stood on the land now occupied by the Catonsville Post Office at 1001 Frederick Road. (Courtesy of the Enoch Pratt Free Library.)

CONTENTS

ACKNOWLEDGMENTS

My deep gratitude goes to my husband, John, and our sons, Matthew, Jared, and Jason. Thank you for giving me time off from my duties as "mom" to write this book.

I would like to thank the follow individuals for their invaluable time and assistance: Jeff Korman, manager, Maryland Department, Enoch Pratt Free Library; Maggie Schorr, president of the Friends of the Catonsville Library, who became an invaluable friend to me; Lisa Vicari, curator of the Catonsville Room; Jean S. Walsh, Catonsville historian extraordinaire and my personal editor; Rebecca Little, babysitter to the "three wise men;" Zachary Vogel for being himself; Louis S. Diggs, author; Lucy Merrill McKean, president, Catonsville Historical Society; my mother, Flora E. Wight, my biggest critic and even bigger fan; and Elizabeth Amey Brown, for pulling me out of a ditch and into an irreplaceable friendship.

I would also like to thank the generous individuals who opened their homes and shared their personal family histories, photographs, and collections with me: Kitty Crider, Catherine Anne "Muzzy" Fisher, John Thornton Hilleary, Scott Trapnell Hilleary, William Hollifield, Stephen Lackey, Pam Kinzel, Trip Riley, Anne Salzman, James Vidmar, and Calvin "Chip" Wiley. Last, but most certainly not least, I would like to thank Antoinette Lawrence Hughes, whose family so graciously posed for the cover of this book 113 years ago.

To the best of my ability, I have attempted to ensure accuracy, given the antiquated and often obscure nature of the subject matter and materials.

REFERENCES

Boblitz, Katherine S. "Catonsville, Remarkable for its Natural Beauty," *The Baltimore Sun*, June 4, 1916.

Brinkmann, Walter. *Never-to-be Forgotten Tales of Catonsville*. Baltimore: Hoffman Brothers Company, 1942.

Diggs, Louis S. *It All Started on Winters Lane: A History of the Black Community in Catonsville, Maryland*. Baltimore: Upton Press, 1995.

Harrison, Marguerite Elton Baker. *There's Always Tomorrow: The Story of a Checkered Life*. New York: Farrar & Rinehart, 1935.

Heidelbach, H. Ralph. *Catonsville's Churches and Schools Before 1950*. Catonsville, MD: Self-published, 1988.

Heidelbach, H. Ralph. *Catonsville's Institutions Before 1950*. Catonsville, MD: Self-published, 1988.

Orser, W. Edward and Joseph L. Arnold. *Catonsville, 1880 to 1940: From Village to Suburb*. Norfolk, VA: The Donning Company, 1989.

INTRODUCTION

As you turn the pages of this book, Catonsville's past does not seem that long ago. You will recognize many buildings and locales that are familiar to you. Your Catonsville is not that much different, in many respects, from the village of over 100 years ago. Many of the residents of the 1880s, or before, lived in the same houses, worshipped at the same churches, and attended the same schools that you do.

Street names will come to mean more to you than, well, just street names. Many streets on which you live and often travel will bring to mind images of people, grand homes, and estates that you will read about in this book. What was once a mundane green metal sign will be a ghost of Catonsville's past in reminders such as Fusting, Hilton, Beechwood, Summit, Oakwood, Ingleside, Kenwood, Bloomsbury, Devere, Keidel, Oak Grove, Gary, Tanglewood, Dunmore, Uplands, Athol, Rosemont, Academy, and Beaumont.

You may read about some locations (Uplands, Athol, Pine Crest, Ventnor Lodge) and say to yourself, "Why, that's in the city, not Catonsville." You are correct by today's boundaries. In 1918, Baltimore City annexed a large section of Baltimore County's eastern border. This was due to county residents wanting to take advantage of city utilities and services. Before 1918, Catonsville extended east on Frederick Road to approximately Augusta Avenue.

In the first chapter, "It All Began with the Catons," you will meet the town's namesake, Richard Caton, and his wife, Mary "Polly" Carroll Caton. Polly's father, Declaration of Independence signer Charles Carroll, can almost be thought of as a "silent partner" in the creation of Catonsville. It was upon his land, not land belonging to Richard Caton, that Catonsville was built. Carroll sent his bankrupt son-in-law to manage the land he owned west of Baltimore City. You could, in some respects, call Catonsville "Carrollsville" and still be accurately reflecting its origin.

The second chapter, "Grand Homes of Catonsville," will take you to a time of great wealth and the halcyon days of the late 1880s and early 20th century, a time before income tax, when a man was able kept every dollar he made. To escape the heat of Baltimore's hot summers, many wealthy families built summer homes in Catonsville. These homes not only served as luxuries, they served as status symbols as well. The rivalry amongst the prosperous homeowners left behind some elegant enhancements to the area. Some have stood the test of time and still stand either as private residences or institutions. Some, sadly, fell in the path of progress, primarily Interstate 695, and were razed. A few remnants remain: a gatepost here, a stone fence there.

You will also meet families who spent a few months out of the year in Catonsville. Some of their fortunes were made in railroads, lumber, transatlantic shipping, chemistry, and banking, just to name a few of their successful endeavors.

The third chapter, "Main Street and Beyond," takes you down Frederick Road, still called "Main Street" by many people today. You will meet the proprietors and their businesses, which served the community then and, in some cases, still do today. The turn-of-the-20th-century real-estate developments of Eden Terrace, Summit Park, Paradise, and Forest Park brought additional well-to-do families, but unlike their summer-dwelling counterparts, they stayed year round. They became the backbone of Catonsville's commerce.

The completion of the Catonsville Short Line Railroad, in 1884, made the burg attractive to middle-income families. A diverse village was born. The post–World War II housing boom brought additional families. Between the years 1880 and 1940, Catonsville went from being a rural village to a modern suburb.

The fourth and fifth chapters, "Hallowed Halls of Learning" and "Houses of Worship," pay tribute to the institutions that make one truly feel that they are a part of a community. Maryland is second only to New York in having the most immigrants settle here. The region had a large German population that was responsible for, among other things, the formation of Salem Lutheran Church in 1849. A German congregation was formed by the assistant rector at St. Timothy's Episcopal Church, Adolph Frost, shortly after it was founded in 1844. Both of these churches, which still stand, are located on Ingleside Avenue.

Schools were attracted to the area due to its healthy, elevated climate and country setting. It gave Baltimore families a place to send their children where they could concentrate on their studies and not be distracted by the hustle and bustle of city life. Many of the schools achieved nationwide accolades—St. Timothy's School for girls and the Roberts-Beach School, to name a couple.

When the Maryland State Hospital for the Insane, now known as Spring Grove Hospital Center, relocated to Catonsville, it began an era of mental health facilities in the area. In chapter six, "Sanitariums," you meet the Gundry family. The Gundrys were a multi-generational family of psychologists who were responsible for most of the areas sanitariums. What appealed to the summer dwellers and educational founders, also, it seems, made for an ideal location for those suffering from mental maladies.

The last chapter, "Faces and Places," is made up of people and images that appealed to me in my research. Many of these stories have never been told before. I hope that you find them interesting as well. Although she died before I was born, I feel as if I made a new friend in Trudy Brosenne after I spent the evening with her sister, looking through her scrapbook and hearing about her life. I hope that you find her story and smile as inspirational as I did.

If this book is your first foray into Catonsville history, then I encourage you to not stop when you turn the last page. Go and explore for yourself, and you just might make a historical discovery of your own! If you are well versed on the subject of Catonsville's history, I hope that I cause you to pause, once or twice, to think, "I never knew that!"

One

IT ALL BEGAN WITH THE CATONS

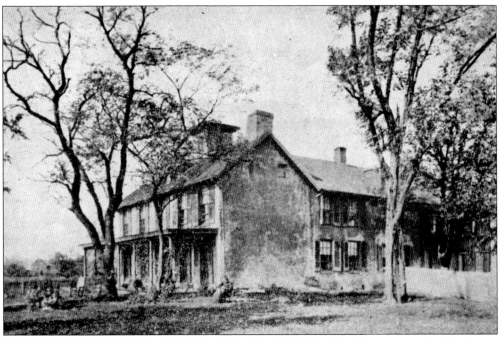

CASTLE THUNDER. The large brick house, built in 1787 on the Frederick Road, was originally the home of Mary "Polly" Carroll, daughter of Charles Carroll, the only Catholic signer of the Declaration of Independence. Polly Carroll married Richard Caton in 1787. When the Baltimore Land Company was terminated in 1810, the land owned by the company was divided among the partners. Charles Carroll's parcels in Baltimore County, west of the city of Baltimore, were named Catonsville, because that land was laid out and developed by Richard Caton, Carroll's son-in-law, who had emigrated from England. The home was located on the corner of Beaumont Avenue and Frederick Road. Castle Thunder was razed in 1903. In 1961, the site became the location of the Catonsville branch of the Baltimore County Public Library. (Courtesy of the Catonsville Room.)

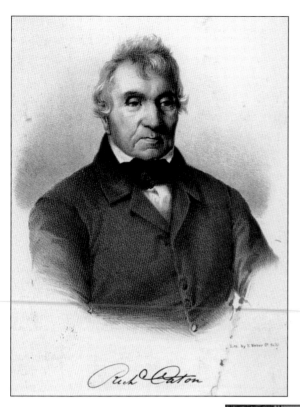

RICHARD CATON (1763–1845). The son of Joseph Caton, Richard was born in Lancashire, England. In 1787, he married Mary Carroll, daughter of Charles Carroll of Carrollton. He had an active and varied business career until he went bankrupt in 1800. He spent his last 40 years as the agent for the Carroll family in their real-estate transactions. (Courtesy of the Enoch Pratt Free Library.)

MARY "POLLY" CARROLL CATON (1770–1846). George Washington is said to have considered her the most beautiful woman he had ever seen. She passed her beauty to her daughters, Mary, Louise, and Elizabeth, known as the "American Graces." They became, respectively, the Marchioness of Wellesley, the Duchess of Leeds, and Lady Stafford. This picture was painted by R. E. Pine. (Courtesy of the Catonsville Room.)

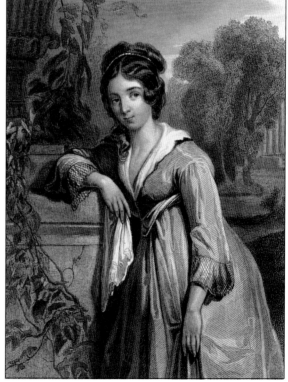

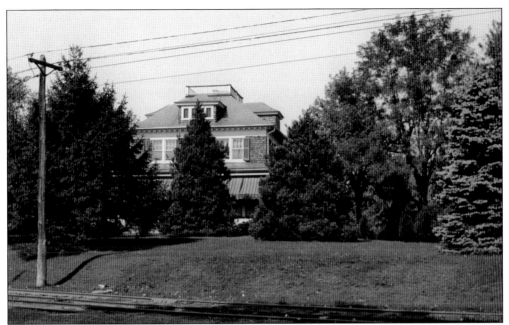

SITE OF CASTLE THUNDER, C. 1936. In 1907, the land was purchased and Castle Thunder was demolished by former senator John Hubner to make way for a hotel. Hubner changed his plans and built a house for Arthur C. Montell, cashier at the First National Bank in Catonsville. It was a two-and-a-half-story frame building with shingled exterior, slate roof, and porches. It was razed in the 1960s, and currently the library occupies the site. (Courtesy of the Enoch Pratt Free Library.)

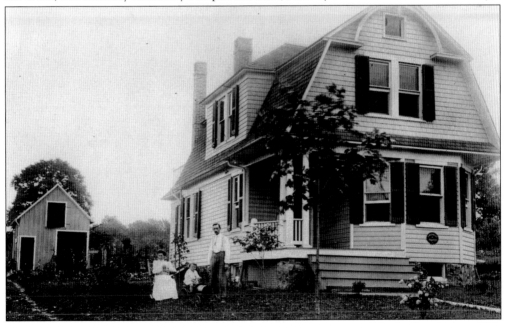

SMITHWOOD AVENUE, NUMBER 119, SUMMER OF 1910. The stone used for the foundation of this house, built in 1905, came from Castle Thunder. The small sign on the front of the house says, "R. Bockmiller. Painter." Pictured here are Barbara Elizabeth (age 43), Leonard (age two months), Richard B. (age one), and Richard R. Bockmiller (age 37). (Courtesy of the Catonsville Room.)

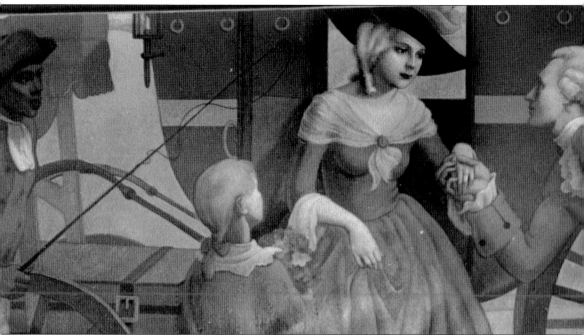

THE HOMECOMING. On December 18, 1936, a mural painted by artist Leonard Bahr was presented to Catonsville High School, then located on Bloomsbury Avenue. Bahr depicts the return of Mr. and Mrs. Caton from their wedding trip to their new home, Castle Thunder. This was one of two murals created by Bahr. The other featured hogsheads filled with tobacco being rolled

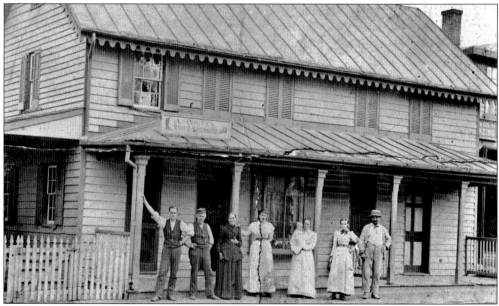

SCHOTTA HOUSE—BOOT AND SHOEMAKERS—825 FREDERICK ROAD. Considering the purchase of this building, John M. Flannigan, shoe repairer, is quoted as saying, "Who would buy that old shack about to fall down?" Evidently, he would, and upon receiving the deed for the premises, he learned that Richard and Mary Caton had built the house and lived there while Castle Thunder was being constructed. (Courtesy of the Catonsville Room.)

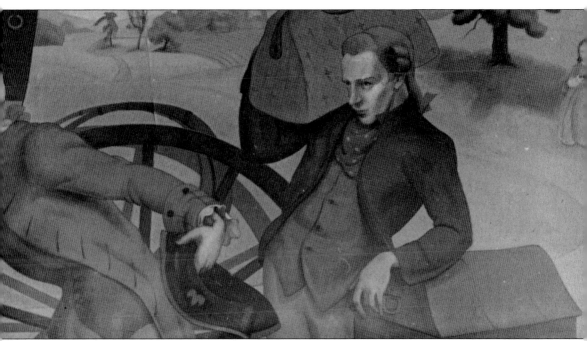

down Rolling Road to Elkridge Landing on the Patapsco River. Unfortunately, the canvasses were destroyed by workmen when the school was renovated and enlarged in the 1960s. (Courtesy of the Enoch Pratt Free Library.)

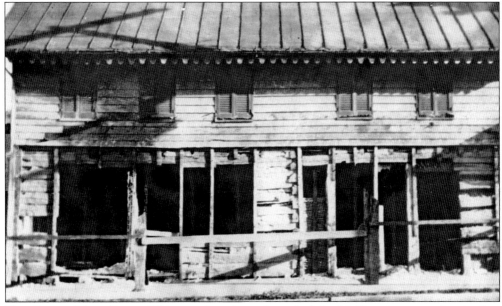

THE CATONS' LOG CABIN. This must have been the sight John M. Flannigan saw when he first laid eyes on his new property. The Catons had built the log cabin as a temporary home while Castle Thunder was being constructed. Although it did not resemble a castle, their new home would outshine the humble cabin with its yellow brick walls, mansard roof, and narrow windows. (Courtesy of the Catonsville Room.)

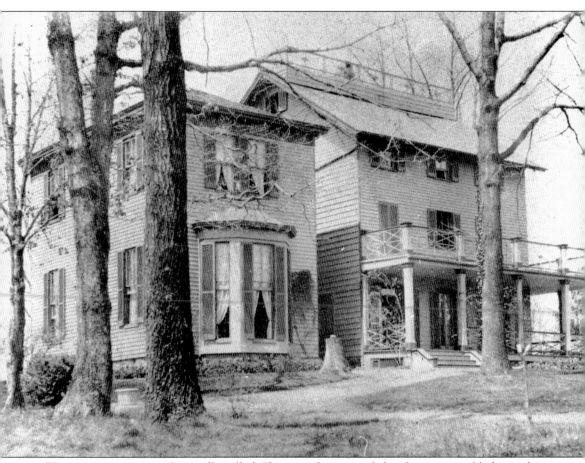

HOMEWOOD, C. 1874. Originally called Chestnut Grove until the chestnut-tree blight in the 19th century, Homewood was built on 52 acres in the 1840s by Joseph P. Fusting. The land was purchased from John S. Gittings for $719.25 (based on inflation, that equals $12,860.55 today). In 1864, Fusting sold part of his property, including his house, to Mrs. Fredericka Karthaus Keidel, the new wife of a German-born widowed physician, Dr. George Frederick William Keidel. They lived there with Dr. Keidel's sons, one of whom (Henry) took possession of the house in 1885. An addition was constructed in 1864 by Dr. Keidel. Additional improvements were made by son Henry in 1900. (Courtesy of the Catonsville Room.)

JOSEPH PHILIP FUSTING (1808–1871). He was born in Hanover, Germany, and came to America at age 21 in 1829. Fusting is considered one of Catonsville founders and major businessmen. As an agent for the horsecar line, he started the flow of people and commerce to the area. He built Chestnut Grove in the 1840s (later called Homewood). He also owned land below and above Homewood and operated a general store on the northwest corner of Frederick Road and Ingleside Avenue (current location of the Coldwell Banker office). (Courtesy of the Catonsville Room.)

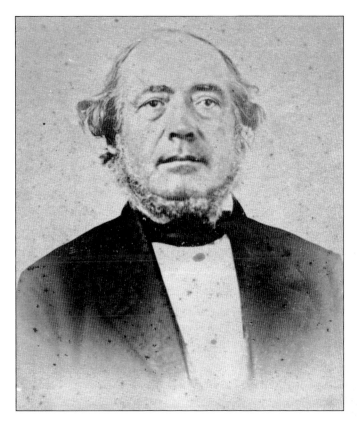

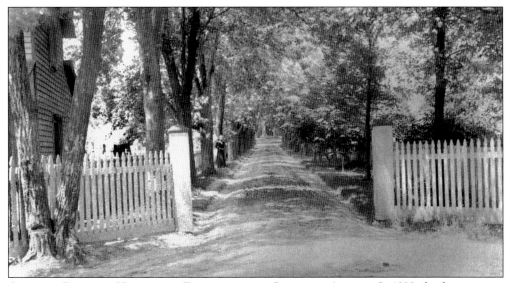

ORIGINAL DRIVE TO HOMEWOOD, ENTRANCE FROM INGLESIDE AVENUE. In 1898, the driveway was extended to Edmondson Avenue after the streetcar tracks and the road were extended westward. Keidel Lane marks the drive's location today. (Courtesy of the Catonsville Room.)

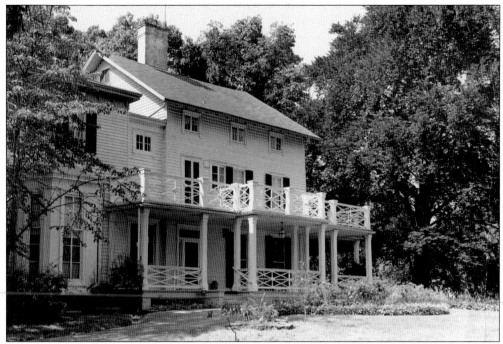

HOMEWOOD—717 EDMONDSON AVENUE. The home is shown here with an addition and improvements made in 1864 and 1900, respectively. In 1935, the house was sold to and occupied by Mr. and Mrs. Irvin B. Spittel and their 18-year-old daughter, Jean. Jean inherited the house and, along with her husband Howard H. Walsh, resided there until 2001. The home still stands and has been subdivided into two apartments. (Courtesy of the Catonsville Room.)

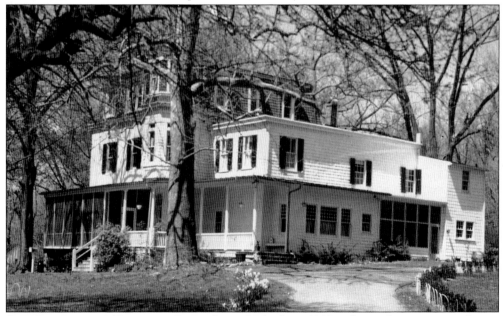

OAK GROVE—1822 FREDERICK ROAD. It was built about 1864 and served as a stagecoach stop for the horsecar line. It is a two-story stone house covered with siding. The house still stands today. (Courtesy of the Catonsville Room.)

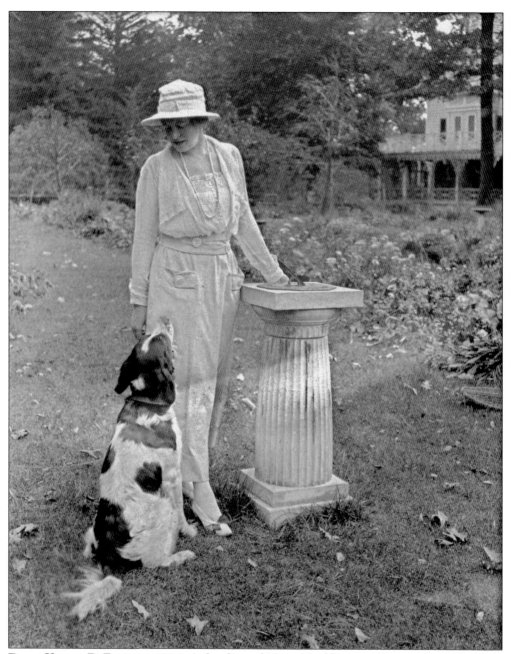

DAISY KEIDEL DEFORD, C. 1914. A daughter of Henry Keidel is seen here in the garden with her faithful animal companion. Homewood can be seen in the background. She later owned the Robin's Range property on North Rolling Road with her husband Louis. Local legend is that Louis, as a boy, once bought a "whole herd" of monkeys for $3.48 each and released them into the trees of Homewood. (Courtesy of the Catonsville Room.)

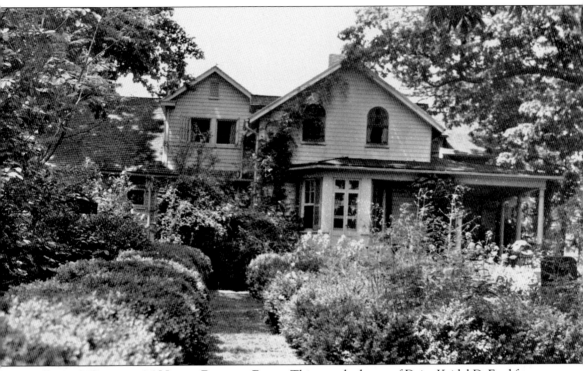

ROBIN'S RANGE—36 NORTH ROLLING ROAD. This was the home of Daisy Keidel DeFord from 1922 to 1947. The house gets its name from the flocks of red-breasted robins that would congregate on the property. The center of the house is a log cabin, built in 1810. It was added on to over the years and lived in by Mrs. Berger, widow of the rector at St. Timothy's, until 1922. The home still stands today. (Courtesy of the Catonsville Room.)

Two

GRAND HOMES
OF CATONSVILLE

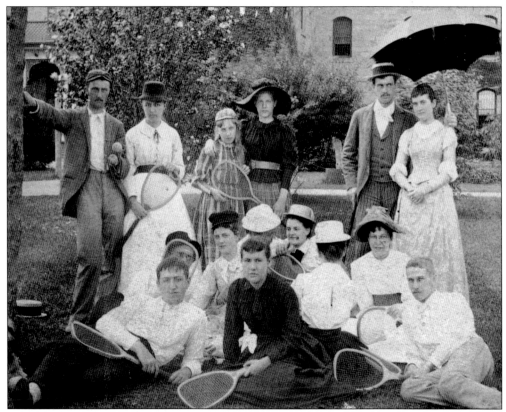

TENNIS AT SPRING GROVE, AUGUST 1890. Pictured from left to right are the following: (first row) Alfred Gundry, Katie Hine, and Harry Krebs; (second row) William Gundry, Numu Ball, unidentified, Grace Gundry, Ella ?, and Helen Krebs; (third row) Bill Phillips, Alice Phillips, Loraine Groverman, Bess Ball, Luther Day, and Isabel Pegle. (Courtesy of the Catonsville Room.)

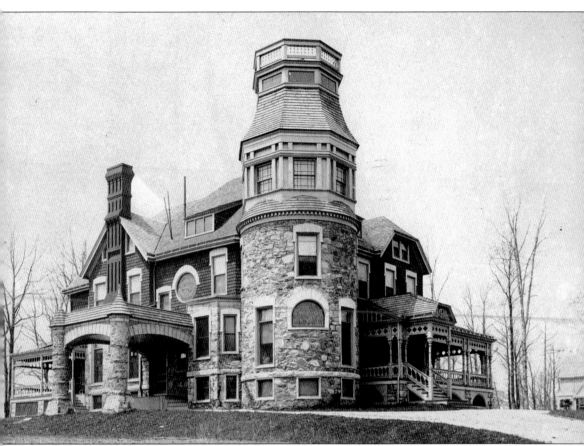

ARDEN. This home was one of the most lavish houses ever constructed in Catonsville, built by Victor G. Bloede in 1898 at an estimated cost of $13,000. The home was the centerpiece of the Eden Terrace community that Bloede's Eden Construction Company developed in the late 1890s. After being among the first graduating class in science at the Cooper Institute in 1868, he went on to make his first fortune by inventing and patenting the glue used on the back of postage stamps. The entrepreneur also owned the Caton Spring Company, the Patapsco Light Company, and the Edmondson Avenue Catonsville & Ellicott City Electric Railway, which supplied utilities to Eden Terrace and transportation for its residents. (Courtesy of the Catonsville Room.)

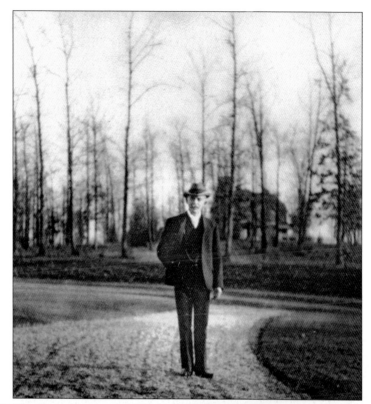

VICTOR GUSTAV BLOEDE (1843–1937). He was the son of Gustav Bloede (d. 1888), a homeopathic physician, and Marie Franziska Bloede (d. 1870), a writer who later used the pseudonym Marie Westland. Bloede's father served as a surgeon in the American Civil War. In 1883, Bloede married Elise Schon. The couple had five children, Marie, Carl S., Ilse, Victor G. Jr., and Vida. (Courtesy of the Catonsville Room.)

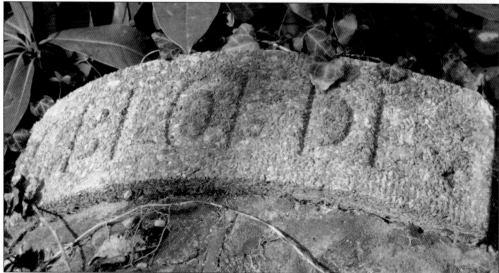

ALL THAT REMAINS OF ARDEN. The house burned on December 22, 1922; the day after, son Victor died of pneumonia. In 1924, Bloede built a stucco house, with a massive copper roof and ballroom, to replace his lost Arden, but it did not come close to replacing its predecessor's beauty and splendor. This fallen entrance marker engraved "Bloede" and its still-erect mate, engraved "Arden," are all that remains of the original mansion, located at the dead end of Forest Avenue in front of the second Arden. This photograph was taken in April 2005. (Courtesy of the author's collection.)

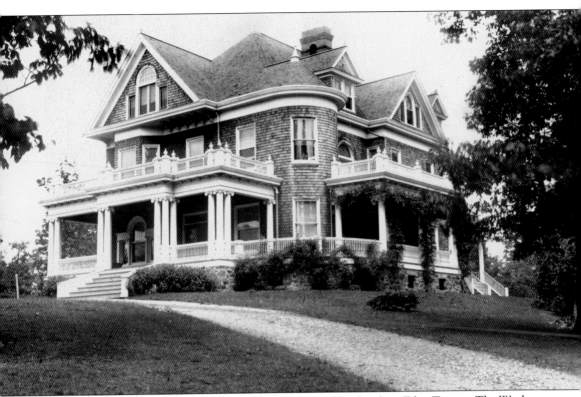

GRAY GABLES. This was the home of Charles Wacker and his family in Eden Terrace. The Wackers were close neighbors, as well as friends, of the Bloedes. Wacker was a partner in the firm of Struven & Wacker, ships' chandlers, in the early 20th century. (Courtesy of the Catonsville Room.)

GRAY GABLES. The daughters of Charles Wacker are shown here on the porch of their home in Eden Terrace. Pictured from left to right are Ilse, Olga, and Carla. (Courtesy of the Catonsville Room.)

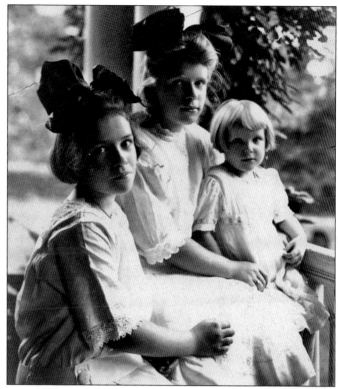

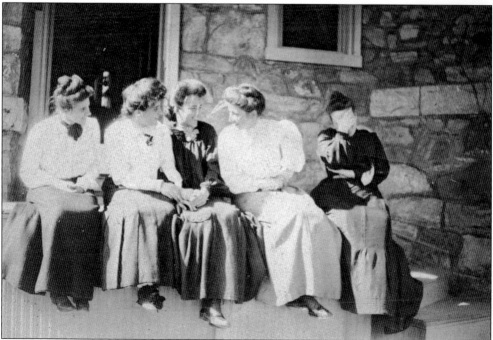

ARDEN PORTE COCHERE. The Wackers and Bloedes were close friends. Pictured from left to right are Lillie E. Wacker, Edna Wacker, Ilse Bloede, Marie Bloede, and Celia Wacker. (Courtesy of the Catonsville Room.)

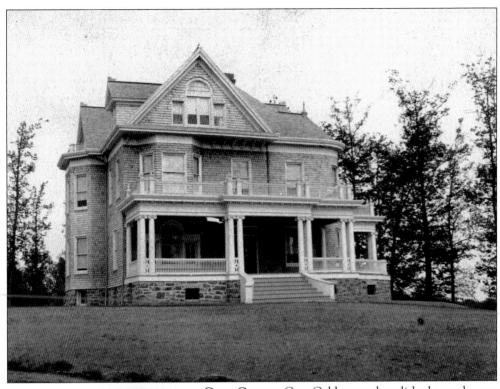

GRAY GABLES. Gray Gables was demolished to make way for the Baltimore Beltway in the early 1960s. (Courtesy of the Catonsville Room.)

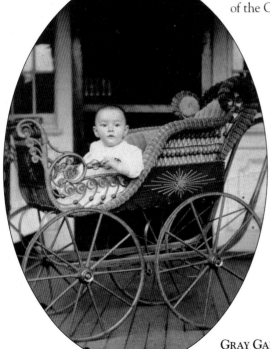

GRAY GABLES. The child in the wicker pram is possibly Carla Wacker. (Courtesy of the Catonsville Room.)

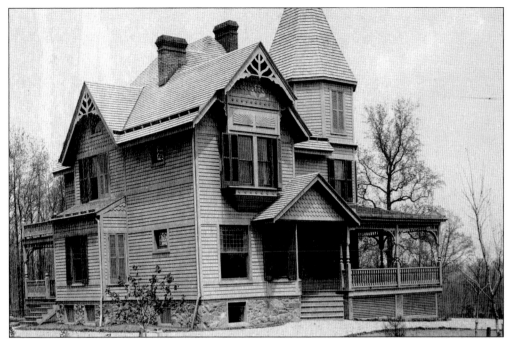

GRIMES HOME—101 ARBUTUS AVENUE, C. 1898. One of the first homes constructed in Eden Terrace, this house was built on lot 20, located on the corner of Woodlawn and Arbutus Avenues. (Courtesy of the Catonsville Room.)

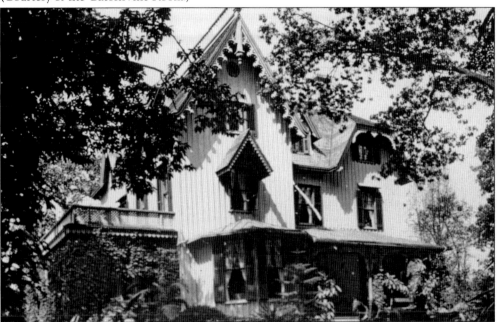

DUNMORE. This home, built by W. J. H. Walters, stood to the east of Eden Terrace. *The Baltimore Sun*, on May 11, 1908, announced that it was to be the new home of the Pot and Kettle Club. A 1915 reference states it was the estate of Frank T. Kirby. The home was a large three-story Victorian with fretted decoration. It was torn down, and in 1941, the community known as Dunmore was developed. (Courtesy of the Catonsville Room.)

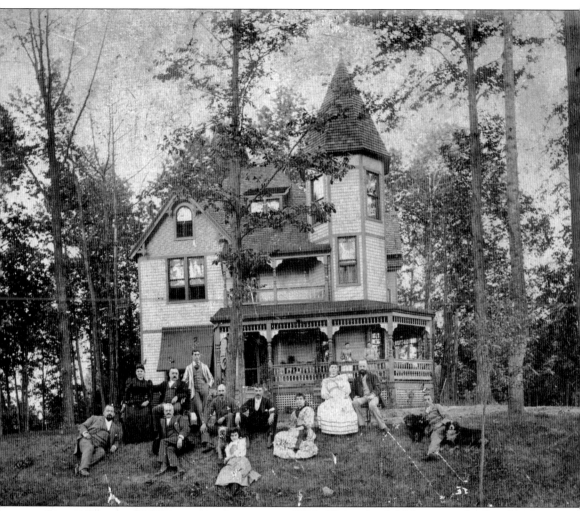

Sucro Home—13 Woodlawn Avenue, c. 1892. This splendid Victorian, the first house built in Eden Terrace, was the home of German immigrant George C. Sucro, manager of the Bartholomew Brewery. He occupied the house, along with his wife, Elizabeth, of Alsace-Lorraine, and their four children. Pictured here are Mr. and Mrs. Sucro (seated on settee on left); their son Fred (standing next to settee); daughter Jennie (seated center with dark hair and dark sash); daughter Antoinette (sitting in foreground on slope); and son William (seated far right, between two dogs). Others in the photograph are unidentified. There are two servants standing on the porch, both German immigrants. The house has been in the family for 113 years. (Courtesy of Antoinette Lawrence Hughes.)

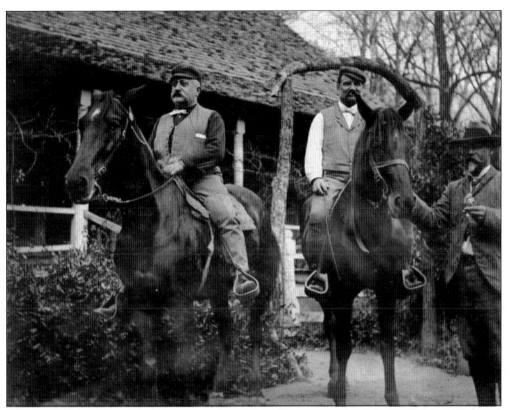

GEORGE SUCRO. Pictured from left to right are George Sucro, manager of the Bartholomew Brewery; Charles Schneider; and an unidentified man. (Courtesy of Antoinette Lawrence Hughes.)

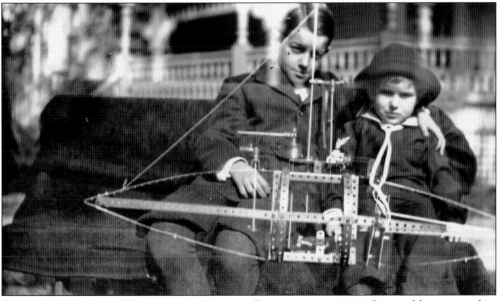

SUCRO GRANDSONS, WILLIAM AND ARTHUR LAWRENCE, C. 1910. Pictured here, seated in front of their grandfather's home at 13 Woodlawn Avenue, are William and Arthur Lawrence. (Courtesy of Antoinette Lawrence Hughes.)

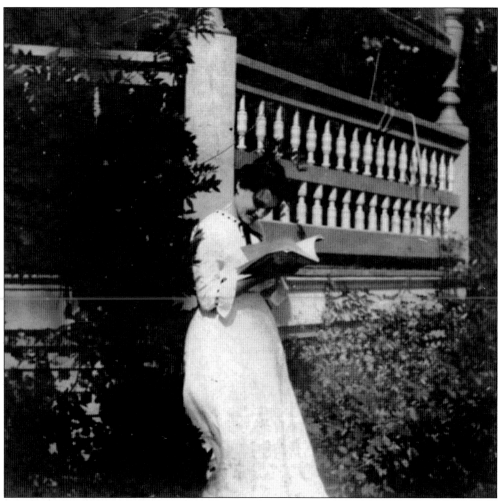

ANTOINETTE SUCRO, C. 1895. Pictured here is the youngest daughter of George and Elizabeth Sucro, Antoinette, reading a book in her summer gown of white. She would later marry Arthur Gower Lawrence and have three children: Arthur, William, and Antoinette. After her parents' death, she, with her husband and children, returned to share the family home on Woodlawn Avenue with her Aunt Jennie. (Courtesy of Antoinette Lawrence Hughes.)

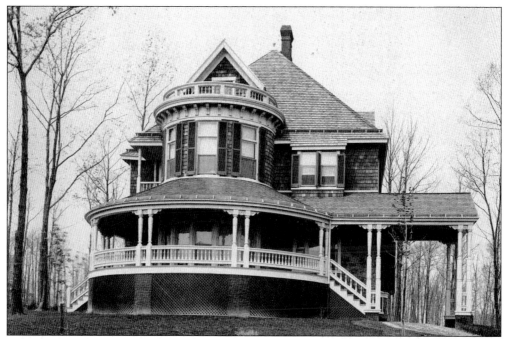

BEVERLY—12 WOODLAWN AVENUE, C. 1893. Beverly was built by H. P. Hall and was one of the original homes in Eden Terrace. Antionette Sucro Lawrence and her husband, Arthur, purchased the home in 1915 from the widowed Mrs. Hall; it was located directly across the avenue from Antoinette's parents. In 1920, the Lawrence family would sell the home to J. E. Downs and move across the street to number 13. (Courtesy of Antoinette Lawrence Hughes.)

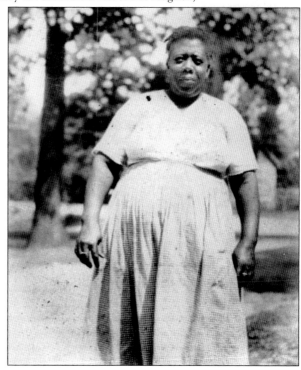

MINERVA RANDALL, C. 1930. She was the laundress to the Sucro family. Minerva lived and raised her 11 children on Winters Lane, where some of her descendents still reside. (Courtesy of Antoinette Lawrence Hughes.)

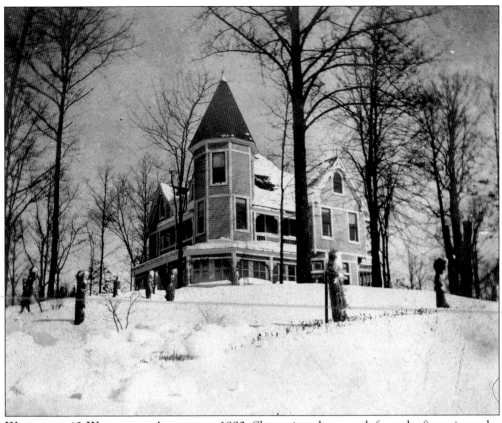

WINTER AT 13 WOODLAWN AVENUE, C. 1893. Shown is a photograph from the first winter the Sucro family spent in their new home. (Courtesy of Antoinette Lawrence Hughes.)

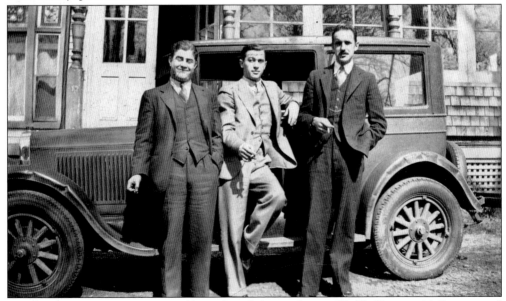

MODEL T FORD, C. 1930. Pictured here, from left to right, are Waddy Hooper, Al Cooper, and Bill Lawrence. (Courtesy of Trip Riley.)

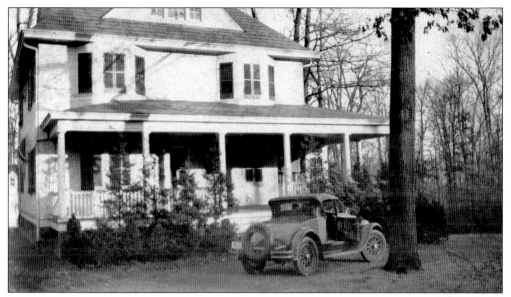

1925 DIANA ROADSTER. The car was owned by J. Russell Riley and is seen here in front of his grandparents' home at 115 Arbutus Avenue. (Courtesy of Trip Riley.)

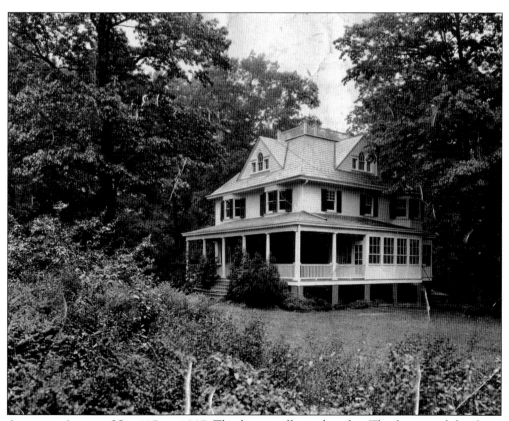

ARBUTUS AVENUE NO. 115, C. 1927. This house still stands today. The front porch has been enclosed. (Courtesy of Trip Riley.)

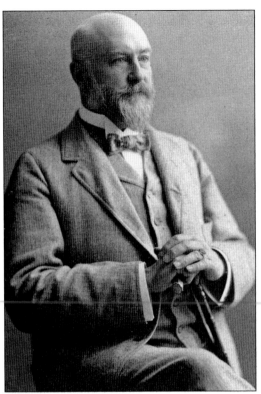

GUSTAV W. LURMAN JR., C. 1896. He fought for the Confederacy in the Civil War and was the son of Gustav W. Sr., a sea merchant, and Frances L. Donnell, who was a descendant of Lady Godiva (as is the author). In 1848, Gustav Sr. purchased the estate known as Bloomsbury Farms, restored its original name, Farmlands, and proceeded to make it a Maryland showplace. (Courtesy of the Catonsville Room.)

FARMLANDS, 1942. This was the name given to the acreage in the late 18th century by Edward Dorsey. The original tract of 2,000-plus acres was later given to his son, Hammond, as a wedding gift. Hammond and his wife built a mansion upon the site. In 1820, the house, with 600 acres, was sold to Henry Sommerville, who renamed it Bloomsbury Farm. (Courtesy of the Enoch Pratt Free Library.)

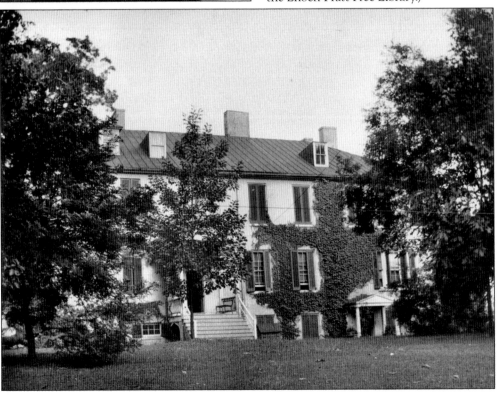

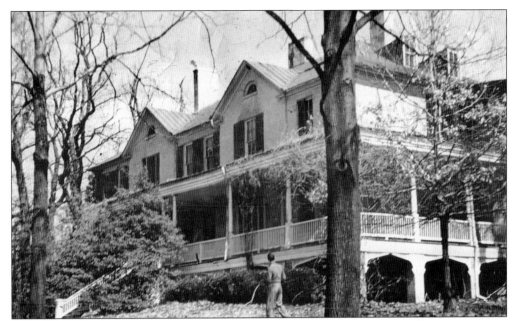

Farmlands, Shortly before It Was Demolished, 1948. In the late 19th century, after Gustav Sr.'s death, most of the property was sold to a cousin and was later returned to Frances Lurman, daughter of Gustav. In 1948, she sold the remaining 65 acres to the board of education for the construction of Catonsville High School. The house was razed, and all that remains are the groundskeeper's cottage and many of the rare trees. This photograph was taken by Virginia Duvall. (Courtesy of the Catonsville Room.)

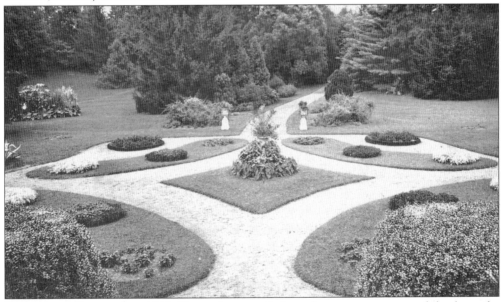

Farmlands Gardens in 1881. Gustav Lurman Sr. brought many rare trees and shrubs to the property. Pictured here is one of only two formal English gardens in the state at the time. While much reduced in scale, the Catonsville High School campus still contains fine examples of bald cypress, dawn redwood, and pond cypress, as well as plum yew, paulownia, and a great gingko tree. (Courtesy of the Catonsville Room.)

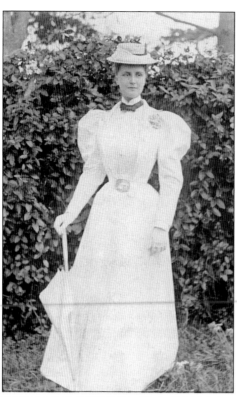

FRANCES "FANNY" LURMAN, C. 1897. She was the daughter of Gustav Jr. and Elizabeth. She was regarded as one of Baltimore's most beautiful women. Although she had many suitors, she declared that she would never marry. "Never" arrived in 1947, when she was in her 70s and a patient at University Hospital in Baltimore. She then married Dorsey W. Williams, a man she first met when she was a teenage girl. She died in 1950, three years after her marriage. (Courtesy of the Catonsville Room.)

THE DEVON HORSE SHOW, MAY 1890. This was possibly in the Catonsville area. Col. Edward Morrell, in top hat and holding a buggy whip, is on the box of his four-in-hand carriage with Fanny Lurman beside him. (Courtesy of the Catonsville Room.)

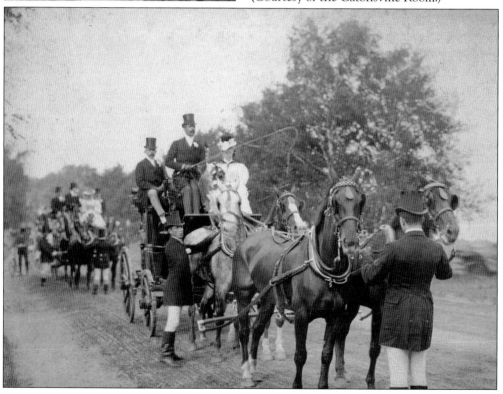

FRANCES "FANNY" LURMAN, 1900. This large painting by Alfred Shriver hangs in Shriver Hall on Johns Hopkins University campus, along with paintings of nine other young Baltimore ladies. (Courtesy of the Catonsville Room.)

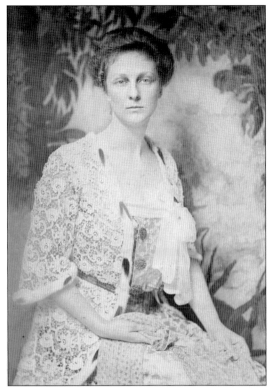

FRANCES LURMAN, TALENTED HORSEWOMAN, C. 1897. Fanny, as she was called, is photographed sitting atop her beloved horse, Tip Top. She won many trophies in both cross-country and hunting riding. (Courtesy of the Catonsville Room.)

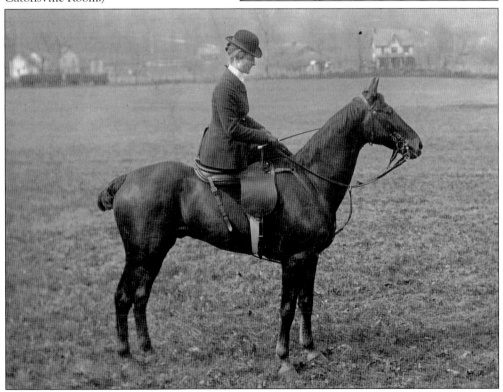

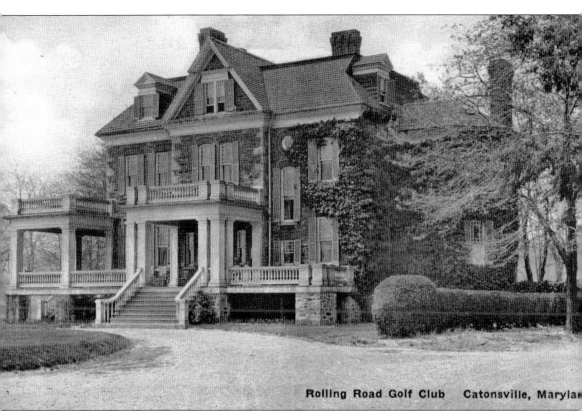

Rolling Road Golf Club   Catonsville, Marylan

BLOOMSBURY, C. 1919. Bloomsbury was built by Gustav Lurman Jr. in 1881 on land he inherited from his father. In 1916, it was acquired as part of the new Rolling Road Golf Club. It was the earliest clubhouse, in continual use from 1919 to 1991, when the club razed the mansion after erecting the current brick clubhouse. (Courtesy of William Hollifield.)

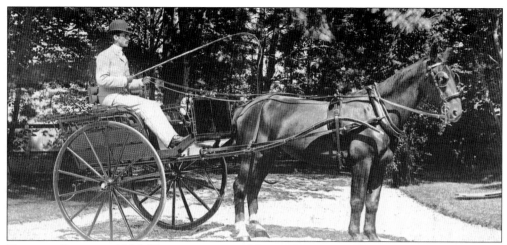

THEODOR LURMAN, 1886. The youngest son of Gustav Sr. is pictured here in one of Bloomsbury's many surreys. (Courtesy of the Catonsville Room.)

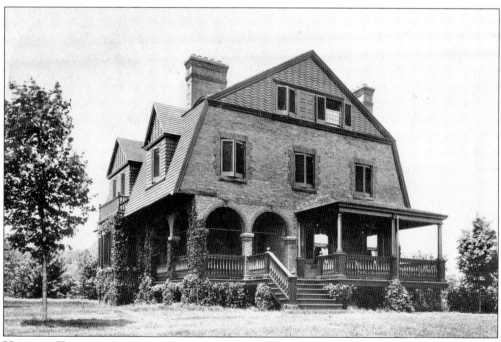

HOME OF THEODOR LURMAN—SOUTH ROLLING ROAD. Lurman was a lawyer, and at different times he owned several sections of the estate of his father, Gustav Lurman Sr. Pictured here is one of his homes. It was designed by architects J. A. and W. T. Wilson. Later, the home became the Rolling Road School (for handicapped children) and now includes offices of the board of education. (Courtesy of the Catonsville Room.)

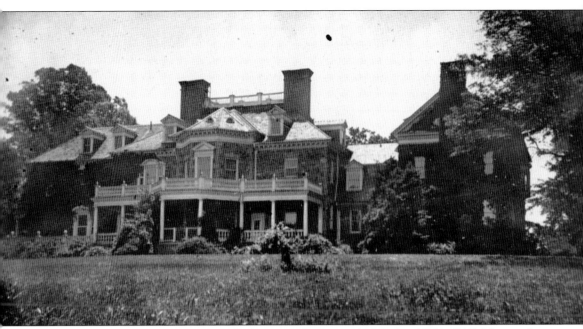

INGLESIDE ESTATE. This estate was built in 1889 by Bernard N. Baker (1854–1918). He was the owner of the Atlantic Transport Line. The mansion was built on land that was occupied by the Ingleside Seminary from 1845 to 1885, when it burned. The 49-room house was designed by architect Henry Randall from a memory Mr. Baker had of a house he had seen in England. By coincidence, Mr. Baker met the English architect of the English house when he was having trouble relaying to the American architect the details of the four-story stairway. The English architect drew the details on Mr. Baker's shirt cuff so that it could be shown to the American architect, Henry Randall. The house was of stone, in the Georgian style of architecture, with terraces, wide verandas, and white pillars. The Bakers had two daughters, Elizabeth and Marguerite. In 1907, Elizabeth married Albert C. Ritchie, who would later become the 49th governor of Maryland. Marguerite was a journalist, international traveler, and a spy for the United States during World War I. Details of her adventurous life can be found in her autobiography, *There's Always Tomorrow*, by Marguerite Elton Baker Harrison (1935). (Courtesy of the Catonsville Room.)

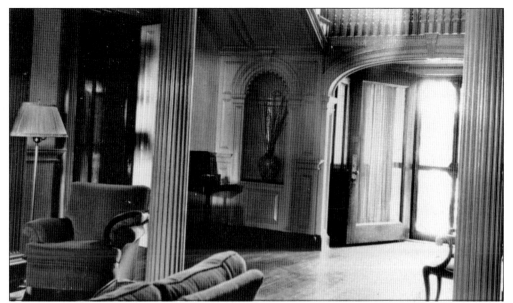

INGLESIDE LIVING ROOM. In her autobiography, Marguerite Baker Harrison recalls her family home: "The dining room and library were paneled in oak, the entrance hall ran the entire length of the house and had a beautiful stairway, pure Georgian in inspiration. There were elaborately carved mantels and parquet floors in all the rooms, and the house boasted nine bathrooms, an almost unheard-of luxury." (Courtesy of the Catonsville Room.)

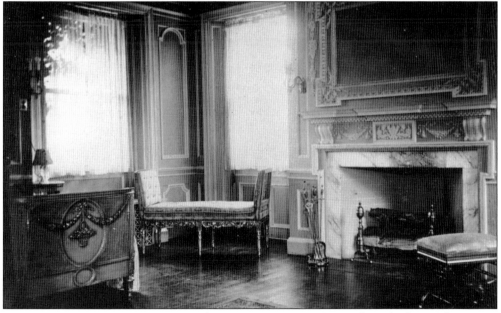

INGLESIDE BEDROOM. Marguerite Baker Harrison wrote, "It was furnished in 18th century English and early American furniture with gay chintz slip covers and upholstery. Long before the craze for antiques and period furniture reached America, my mother had begun to discard the dreadful upholstered plush and brocade atrocities of the eighties and nineties and to replace them with beautiful and simple lines of Chippendale, Sheraton and Duncan Phyfe." (Courtesy of the Catonsville Room.)

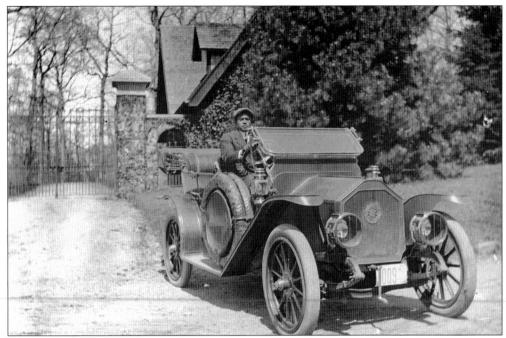

INGLESIDE GATEHOUSE, 1912. When asked about his gatehouse, Mr. Baker said, "Every proper English estate has a gatehouse and gatekeeper to wave to the family as they come and go." Pictured here is a 1908 Pierce-Arrow being driven by a Catonsville resident named Siecke. (Courtesy of the Catonsville Room.)

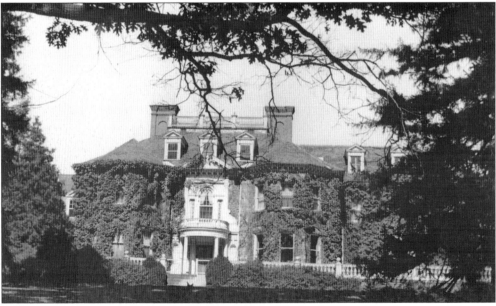

INGLESIDE ESTATE, 1942. Mr. Baker died in 1918, and Ingleside was sold to Antonio T. Carozza, a prominent contractor on large public works throughout the East. In the 1930s, it was used by several families who rented certain areas of the tremendous mansion. It was gutted by fire in 1953. Westview Shopping Center is now located on the site. (Courtesy of the Enoch Pratt Free Library.)

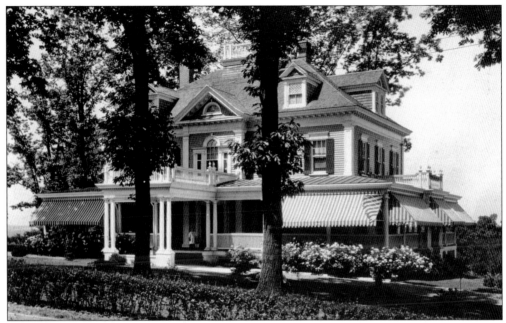

FAIRLEE—10 SEMINOLE AVENUE. Fairlee was built in 1897 by F. Marion McComas. Families that have subsequently owned the house are Valiant, Moscas, Maher, and Whelan. (Courtesy of the Catonsville Room.)

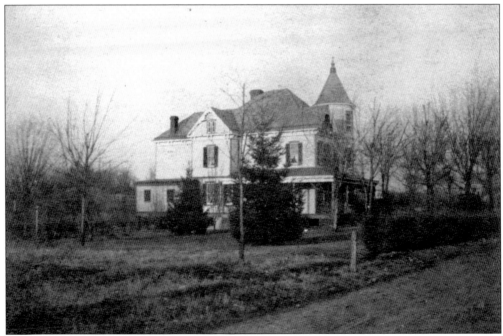

HOME OF IDA CULLIMORE FRANCE—117 MELVIN AVENUE. This home, located on the southwest corner of Melvin and Edmondson Avenues, was built by the widow of Jacob France II, founder of the France, Southcomb Hat Company in Baltimore in 1890. It still stands today. (Courtesy of the Catonsville Room.)

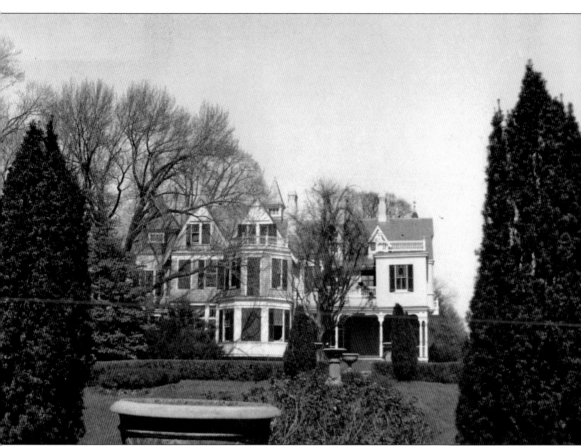

UPLANDS MANSION—4501 OLD FREDERICK ROAD, C. 1940. This was the "spring" home of Mary Sloane Frick Garrett Jacobs. She wintered at her home at 11 West Mount Vernon Place (now the Engineers Club) and summered in Newport, Rhode Island. She was considered the social arbiter of Baltimore for many years and entertained in a truly regal manner said to have been unequalled by any Baltimore hostess and comparable with those in New York and Newport, Rhode Island. Mrs. Jacobs inherited the home from her father, William Frick. This acreage formed part of the 17th-century estate of "Hector's Fancy" and was once called "Bleake Hill." Uplands originally was designed by William H. Reasin and was remodeled to its present design by E. Francis Baldwin, both prominent 19th-century architects. Mrs. Jacobs bequeathed Uplands to the Episcopal Diocese of Maryland to become a home for elderly ladies in reduced circumstances. Currently the house is in jeopardy of being razed to make room for the new Uplands Development. (Courtesy of the Enoch Pratt Free Library.)

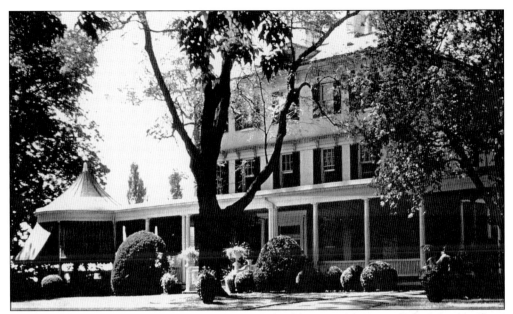

BELLEVUE. This home was last owned by R. Howard Bland (1880–1959), Harvard Law School graduate and former president of the U.S. Fidelity and Guarantee Company. In 1930, he served as president of the Spring Grove Hospital board of managers. The Bland-Bryant Convalescent Building still bears his name. The home was razed preceding the purchase of the property by the YMCA to build its Western facility, located at 850 South Rolling Road. (Courtesy of the Catonsville Room.)

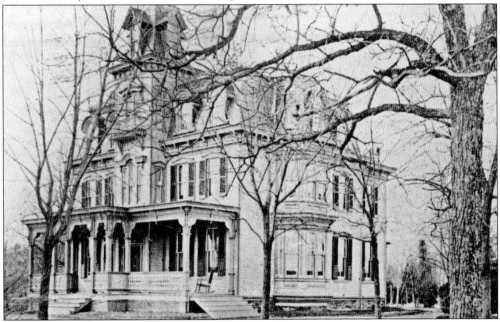

BEECHWOOD MANSION. This was the home of state senator John Hubner, who moved to Catonsville in 1870 and served in the Maryland House of Delegates and State Senate off and on between *c.* 1880 and 1910. He was an active real-estate developer in Catonsville. Catonsville Presbyterian Church was built on the front lawn of the house in 1921, when it was owned by the Coblentz family. The house was razed in 1963 for an extension of the church. (Courtesy of the Catonsville Room.)

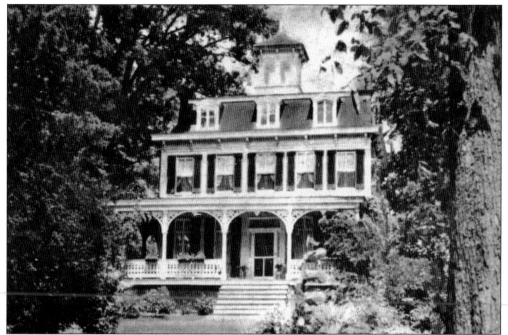

THE POPLARS, BUILT IN 1864. This was the home of George Helfrich on Frederick Road, near Nunnery Lane and west of Overbrook Road. In the 1850s, Helfrich established a lumber business in Baltimore. (Courtesy of the Catonsville Room.)

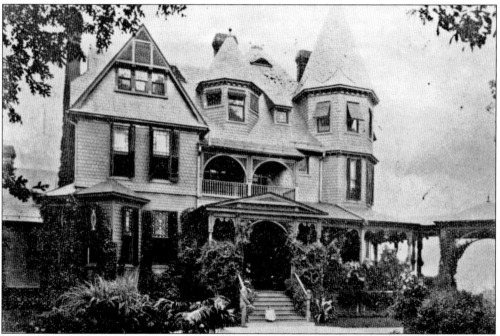

TANGLEWOOD. This was the home of Wesley M. Oler in 1894. Oler was in the ice and coal business, or ,as he liked to say, summer and winter. Pres. Theodore Roosevelt was once a guest of the Olers. The house was razed in the 1930s for the development of the Tanglewood community, located south of Frederick Road and Maiden Choice Lane. (Courtesy of the Catonsville Room.)

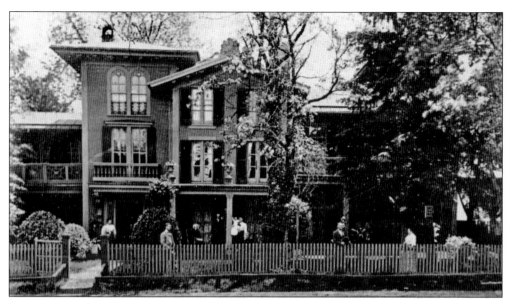

EUREKA, C. 1894. Here is the home of Dr. Charles G. W. MacGill in Catonsville. Dr. MacGill, originally from Hagerstown, was the regimental surgeon of the famous 2nd Virginia Brigade of Infantry, Stonewall Bridge, during the Civil War. The Italianate house underwent numerous renovations before achieving the appearance seen in this photograph. Located near Frederick Road and Bishop's Lane, it was razed around 1950 and replaced by a gas station. (Courtesy of the Catonsville Room.)

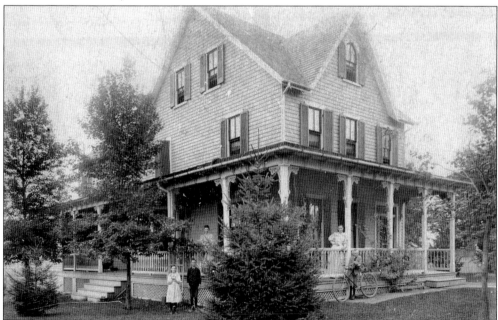

NEWBURG AVENUE, NO. 105, BUILT IN 1901. Shown here is the home of John S. Wilson, co-owner of Wilson & Poehlmann Lumber & Coal. Pictured on the left side of the photograph are Mrs. MacCubin, a guest (standing on the porch); Miss Ethel Wilson and cousin, Charles Mirnick (on the ground); and, on the right side of the photograph, Mrs. Wilson (on the porch) and Bert Nelson (leaning on bicycle). The home still stands. (Courtesy of the Catonsville Room.)

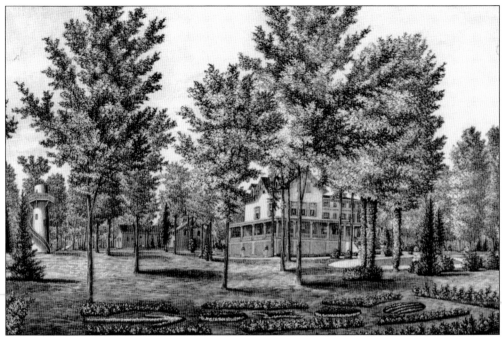

TOWER HILL. This was the residence of Henry James, president of Citizens National Bank and lumber tycoon. Born in Truxton, New York, in 1821, he moved to Maryland as a young man. Besides his banking endeavors, he owned several lumber mills in Pennsylvania and Maryland. The estate was located on the northwest corner of Frederick and North Bend Roads. It was razed for the development of Jamestown Court. (Courtesy of the Catonsville Room.)

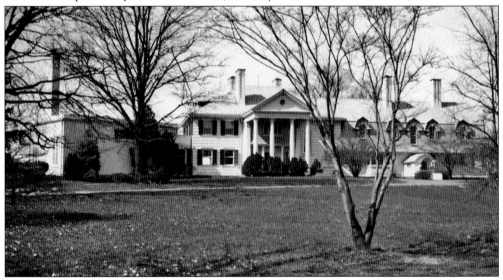

OVERHILLS MANSION—916 SOUTH ROLLING ROAD. This home was built in 1897 by Henry James as a wedding present for his son Norman and his bride, Margie MacGill, daughter of the Civil War doctor. Overhills is a showcase of imported and domestic hardwoods, from its egg-and-dart and dentil motifs, to the fruitwood and teak paneling in the ballroom (added in the 1920s), to the massive columns that support the portico. It is currently being used as a meeting and wedding facility. (Courtesy of the Catonsville Room.)

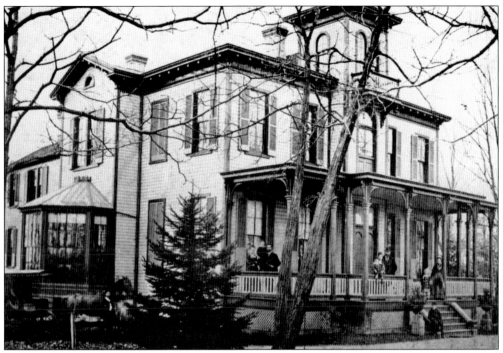

WALDECK—736 EDMONDSON AVENUE. Built in the 1870s by John Fefill, it was originally called Stratford. The estate was purchased in 1877 as a summer home by Gustav and Auguste Gieske, who renamed it. Waldeck means "woods corner." Gieske, a native of Oldenburg, Germany, became a Baltimore tobacco dealer. It is now the Sterling-Ashton-Schwab Funeral Home and sits on six acres of the original estate. (Courtesy of the Catonsville Room.)

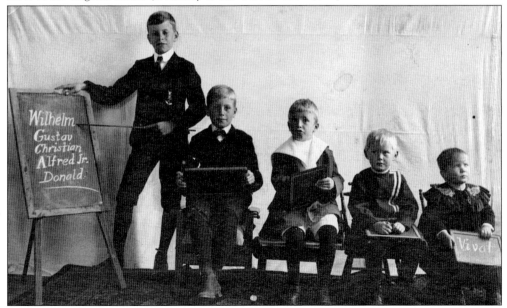

PLAYING SCHOOL AT WALDECK, C. 1905. Pictured here, from left to right, are Wilhelm Lentz, Gustav Lentz, Christian Lentz, Alfred Gieske Jr., and Donald Gieske. (Courtesy of the Catonsville Room.)

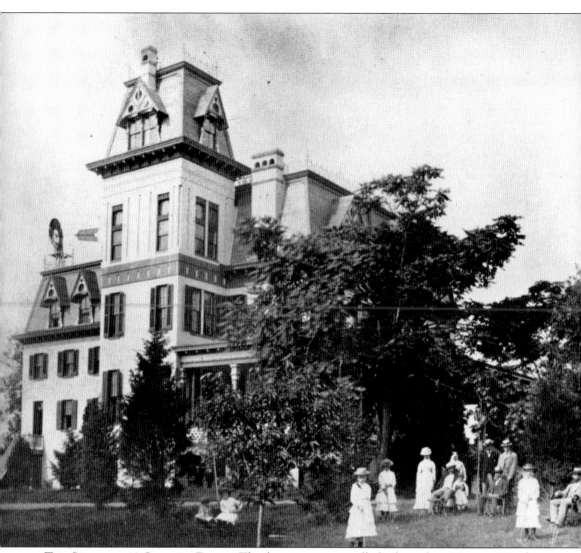

THE SUMMIT—10 STANLEY DRIVE. This house was originally built in the 1850s or 1860s for Charles and Margaret Koefoed so that their sons could attend St. Timothy's School for Boys and their daughters the Patapsco Institute. Mrs. Koefoed and the children lived in the gatehouse while waiting for the house's completion, which was halted during the Civil War. Union troops are believed to have camped on the property. Mr. Koefoed, a Danish consul to the West Indies, died before the house's completion, and his wife, never having lived in it, sold it to James A. Gary. The 100-acre estate became Gary's summer home. The estate was sold in 1919 and subdivided into a middle-income housing community called Summit Park by Mohler Brothers Real Estate. The mansion was placed on the National Register of Historic Sites in 1979. (Courtesy of the Catonsville Room.)

JAMES ALBERT GARY (1833–1920). He ran unsuccessfully for the U.S. House of Representatives in 1870 but served for 24 years as a delegate to the Republican National Convention. Gary also ran unsuccessfully in 1880 for the governorship of Maryland. Gary accepted an offer by President McKinley to become postmaster general in 1897. Gary served for just over a year. He resigned his post on April 18, 1898, due to both health reasons and opposition to impending hostilities with Spain. This photograph is from a portrait in the possession of E. S. Gary. (Courtesy of the Enoch Pratt Free Library.)

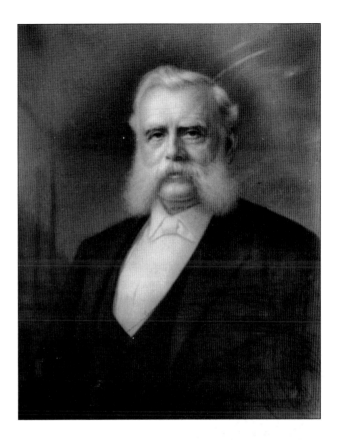

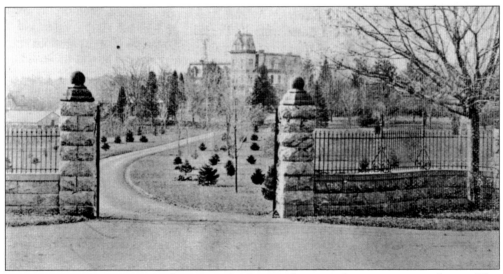

THE SUMMIT, C. 1895. Since the 1920s, the Summit has served as an apartment house. This drawing is from D. B. Perkins's book, *Picturesque Catonsville*, published in 1895. The gates shown here were sold to Manresa-on-the-Severn in Annapolis, which served as a Catholic retreat house from 1914 to 1964. Today it is the home of Atria Manresa, a retirement community. (Courtesy of the Catonsville Room.)

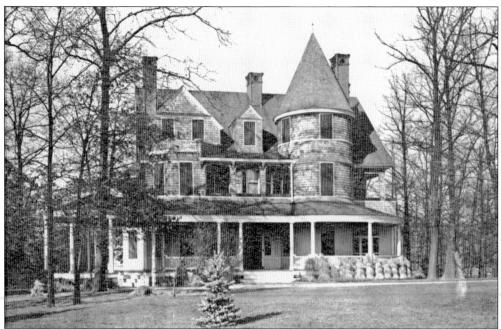

OAKWOOD, 1300 SUMMIT AVENUE. In 1894, August H. Brinkmann, president of the Baltimore Corset and Novelty Works, purchased a large lot and started construction of a summer house the following year. Brinkmann hired Baltimore contractor Milton C. Davis to construct the three-story frame Queen Anne building at a cost of $20,000. It was placed on a very broad and deep lot. It is shown here with its shutters closed for the winter. (Courtesy of the Catonsville Room.)

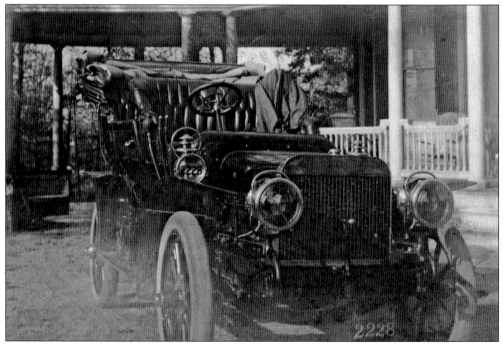

BRINKMANN'S AUTOMOBILE, C. 1904. Pictured here is a pre–World War I touring car with an English-style steering wheel placement. (Courtesy of the Catonsville Room.)

WALTER AUGUST BRINKMANN C. 1925. He was a sportsman and a gifted storyteller. He wrote two books, *Never-to-be Forgotten Tales of Catonsville* and *Now Let's Laugh*. He was the son of August Brinkmann. (Courtesy of the Catonsville Room.)

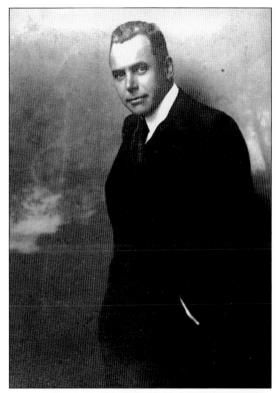

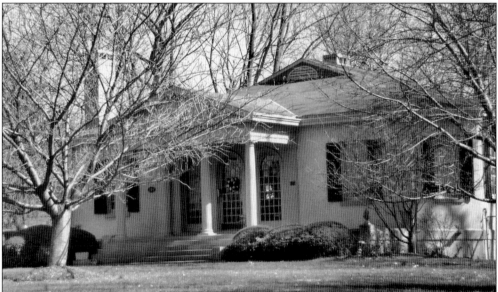

BRINKMANN HOUSE—1301 EDMONDSON AVENUE. Walter Brinkmann lived here from 1921 until 1948. The house is unique to Catonsville. The "concrete bungalow," as it was called at the time, was designed by noted Baltimore architects Wyatt & Nolting in 1910. The main block of the house, with a projecting pediment portico and octagonal ends, seems to be loosely suggestive of Thomas Jefferson's Monticello in Virginia. The house remains in the Brinkmann family. (Courtesy of the author's collection.)

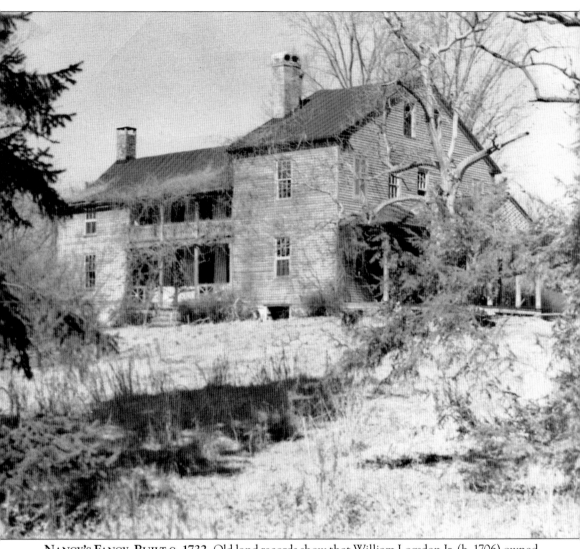

Nancy's Fancy, Built c. 1732. Old land records show that William Logsdon Jr. (b. 1706) owned a track of land listed as "Nancy's Fancy on Hunting Ridge." In 1729, he married Ann Davis, whose father, Henry, was originally granted the land. Sometime before 1880, Edward Spencer (1824–1883) and Anne Catherine "Braddie" Bradford Harrison Spencer (d. 1882) purchased the property. Edward was a writer and dramatist who wrote, at times, for the *Baltimore Bulletin* and the *Sun*, and he wanted to be close to Baltimore City. Braddie was a salon photographer. The Spencers died in the early 1880s of tuberculosis and left the care of their four children to a woman named Eliza Benson, an African American woman and a freed slave who had once been owned by Braddie Harrison. Nan Hayden Agle, granddaughter of the Spencers, wrote a book about Eliza's life called *A Promise Is to Keep*. The estate was located on the corner of Edmondson Avenue and Nunnery Lane (now called Academy Road). Built around an old log cabin, it was a large house, with 13 rooms and as many fireplaces. (Courtesy of the Catonsville Room.)

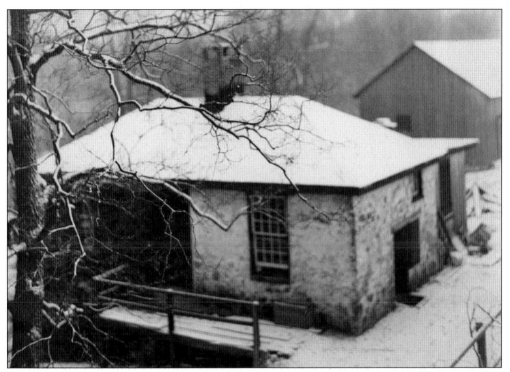

STONE HOUSE AT NANCY'S FANCY. The old building on the property was most likely erected by the Logsdons in 1732. Near the old stone house was a graveyard. One headstone indicated that "Catherine Kroft was massacred." The graves were moved to another cemetery. Nancy's Fancy was razed in 1970 when the Christian Temple Church was built at 5820 Edmondson Avenue. This photograph was taken by Emily Spencer Hayden. (Courtesy of the Enoch Pratt Free Library.)

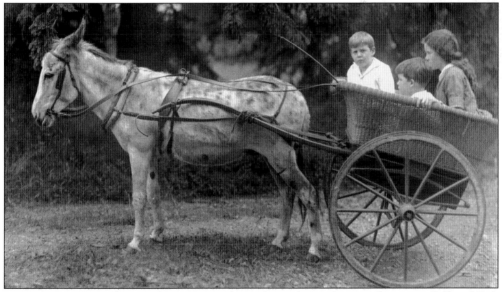

NAN HAYEN AGLE (B. 1905), C. 1912. She is shown here, along with cousins Bill and Bob Alleman, being pulled by Peanuts. Nancy's Fancy had an apple orchard, pine and black walnut trees, and a spring. (Courtesy of the Catonsville Room.)

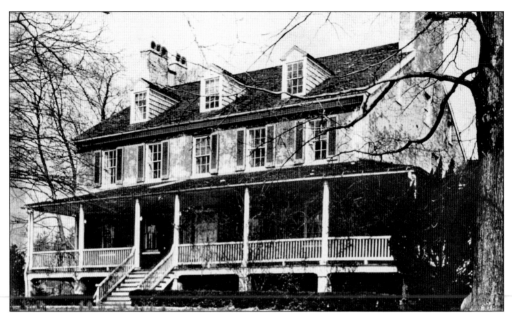

HILTON, C. 1917. This house is located on what was an 1,800-acre tract known as Taylor's Forest in 1678. The mansion was most likely constructed and named by John Buchanan, owner in the late 1820s. By 1842, the property, greatly reduced in size, was used as a summer home by Judge John Glenn. The mansion is seen here right before 1917 renovations. (Courtesy of the Catonsville Room.)

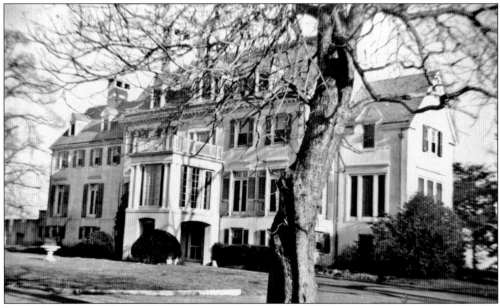

HILTON, C. 1920. In 1917, it was purchased by Col. George W. Knapp, who made major renovations and additions to the estate. He repaired the bowling alley and cottages. The porch faced toward Annapolis, where no buildings, even as late as 1972, obstructed the view of valleys and woodlands. Now the administrative building of Catonsville Community College is located here. The house was placed on the National Register of Historical Places in 1980. (Courtesy of the Catonsville Room.)

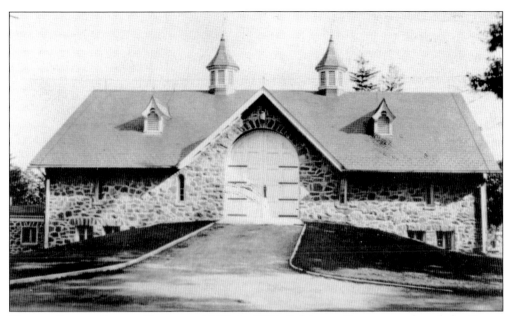

HILTON STONE CATTLE BARN, C. 1925. In 1962, Baltimore County purchased the Knapp estate for Catonsville Community College. The cattle barn is now home to the college's theater and thespian group, the Barnstormers. This photograph is by Jean S. Walsh. (Courtesy of the Catonsville Room.)

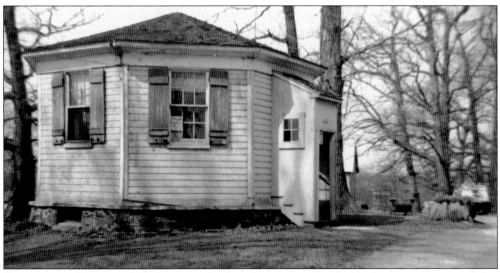

OCTAGONAL HOUSE, 1957. Legend tells that slaves were checked in here and auctioned, but records show that only 26 slaves, in eight families, were owned by the Glenns. There is also a small slave graveyard. Later this housed the dairy office. The mansion was used as a base to smuggle British newsmen into the Confederacy during the Civil War. After the war, it is reported that both Jefferson Davis and Robert E. Lee were guests at Hilton. (Courtesy of the Catonsville Room.)

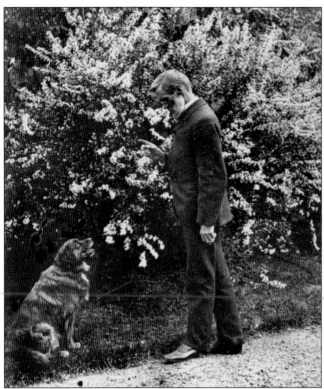

Dr. William Simon, c. 1890. Dr. Simon was a professor of chemistry at the University of Maryland School of Pharmacy for 30 years. The school still gives out a prize in his name to a student who shows superior work in the field of biomedicinal chemistry. (Courtesy of the Catonsville Room.)

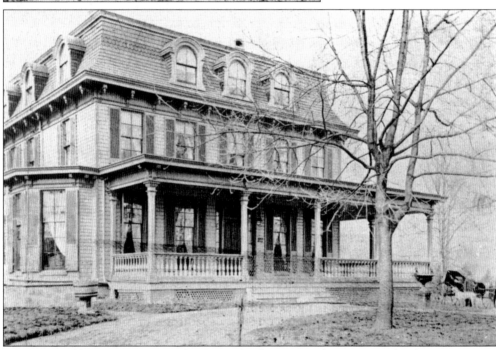

Dr. Simon's Home, 1890. Located at 311 Ingleside Avenue, the once grand Italianate mansion currently is home to Forest Haven Nursing Home. A map of 1877 shows that the land, with a house on it, belonged to "M. Pusey," possibly Mary Marsh Pusey. (Courtesy of the Catonsville Room.)

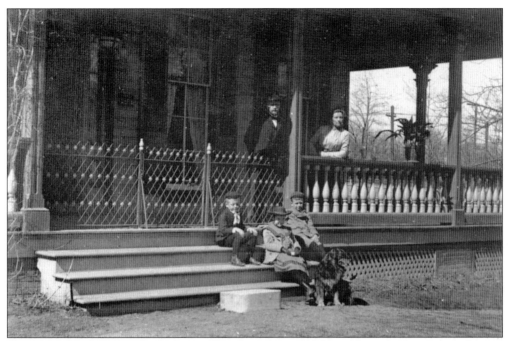

DR. AND MRS. SIMON AND CHILDREN/GRANDCHILDREN. Notice the stepping-stone in front to get into carriages. (Courtesy of the Catonsville Room.)

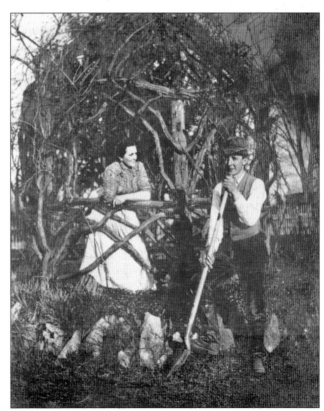

DR. SIMON'S GARDENER AND MRS. CADEGAN IN GAZEBO. Note the natural bent-wood design of this primitive yet elegant gazebo. (Courtesy of the Catonsville Room.)

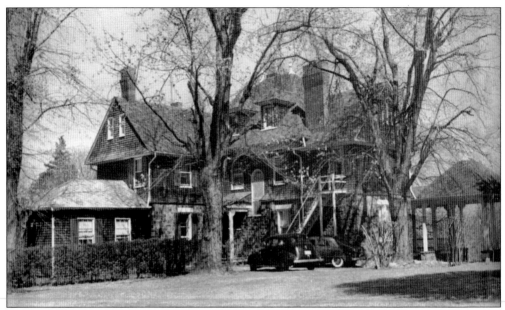

VENTNOR LODGE, C. 1950—526 SOUTH CHAPEL GATE LANE. This house was built in 1890 by James Whiteley, owner of the Whiteley Tug Boat Company and co-founder of the Rolling Road Golf Club, as a summer home. In 1936, Julia Dorsey, first wife of Hammond P. Dorsey, who lived next door at Hammond Hall, purchased Ventnor and turned it into a nursing home, which closed in 1968. In 1979, it was reopened as a domiciliary care facility. (Courtesy of Scott Trapnell Hilleary.)

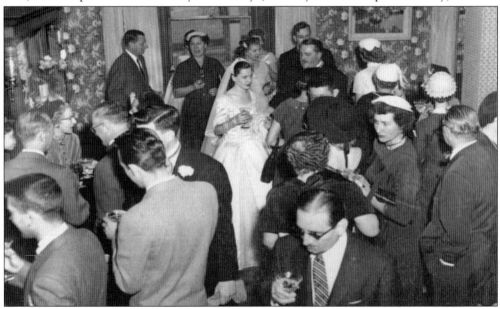

WEDDING AT VENTNOR LODGE, 1956. The Dorseys' son Hammond B. wed Gisela Bergmann of Bavaria at Ventnor Hall. Pictured here are the bride and groom (at center); Julia Dorsey (with tight curls and her back to the camera); Eleanor "Polly" Trapnell Hilleary (center right in profile with white hat), future second wife of Hammond P.; and Frank Lancelotta (with a martini in his hand in foreground), owner of the Wyndhome estate and Victorian mansion, which adjoins the Ventnor property. (Courtesy of Scott Trapnell Hilleary.)

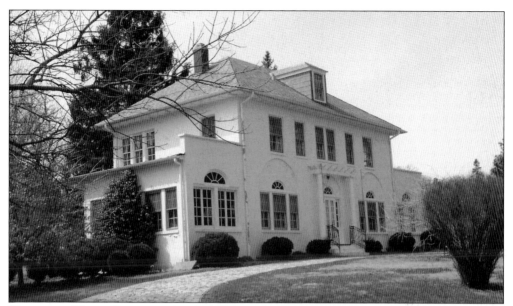

Hammond Hall, Built 1924—602 South Chapel Gate Lane. This home was built by Hammond P. Dorsey on a portion of the Pine Crest Sanitarium property given to him by his aunt, Anna A. Sieling (see page 112). Currently the house is occupied by Scott T. Hilleary, the proprietor of Ventnor Lodge. In 1994, Mrs. Eleanor T. Hilleary Dorsey Dosh had 20 acres permanently preserved in perpetuity by the Maryland Environmental Trust in memory of her late husband. (Courtesy of the author's collection.)

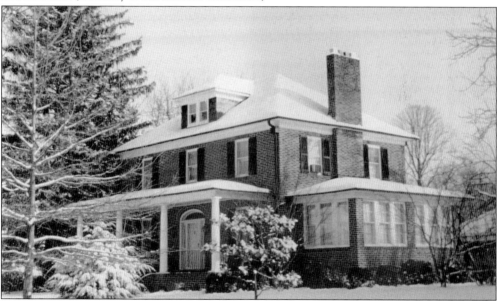

Kalb Home, Built 1928—101 Fairfield Drive. This home was built by William Kalb, owner of the Kalb Pottery. In 1967, it was purchased by Eleanor T. Hilleary Dorsey Dosh. The willow oak in the foreground was from a seedling planted by Lady Bird Johnson at the White House. J. Thornton Hilleary, son of Mrs. Dosh, was a landscape gardener at the White House at the time. He authored the book *My Thousand Days at the President's House* and resides in the home today. (Courtesy of John Thornton Hilleary.)

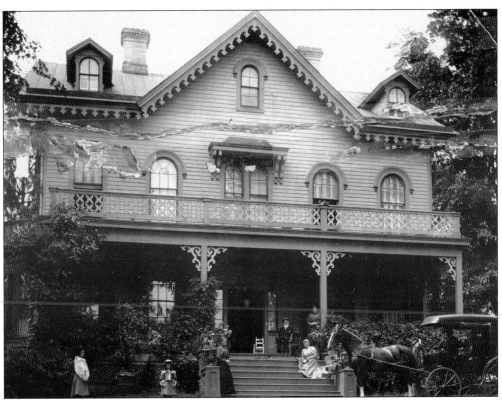

HERNDON, BUILT ABOUT 1850. This was the home of Benjamin Whiteley (d. 1907), wholesale dry-goods merchant, who died at his home on North Bend and Frederick Road. He was the son of Dr. William Whiteley and grandson of Col. William Whiteley, an American Revolution patriot. (Courtesy of the Catonsville Room.)

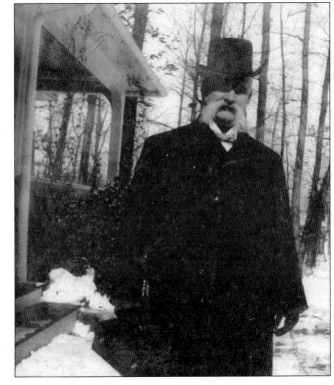

DR. WILLIAM WHITELEY. Dr. Whiteley was the son of Col. William Whiteley, an American Revolution patriot. (Courtesy of the Catonsville Room.)

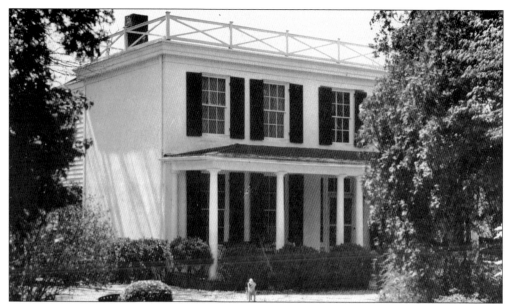

ROSEMONT—28 MAPLE AVENUE. This home was owned by the Schlenkers during the 20th century. In the 1930s, the gabled roof burned during a bootlegging arrest in the years when federal law prohibited the manufacturing and consumption of alcohol. The bootleggers set the fire when prohibition agents were reported to be coming to inspect the house. The Fernandez family owned the property for a long period before the Schlenkers bought it in the 1960s. (Courtesy of the Catonsville Room.)

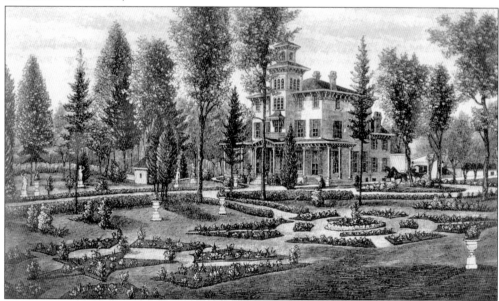

BELLE GROVE—DARIUS CARPENTER HOWELL HOUSE—11 BELLE GROVE ROAD, BUILT 1849. This estate ran from Frederick Road to Taylor's Lane. When bought by the Preston family around 1912, the estate comprised about 42 acres. Subsequently, it was sold to George Kimberley, and after that to a Miss Cole who used the house and, by then, much reduced estate as a nursing home. Today it has been returned to use as a private home. This sketch appears in Thomas Scharf's *History of Baltimore County and City.* (Courtesy of the Enoch Pratt Free Library.)

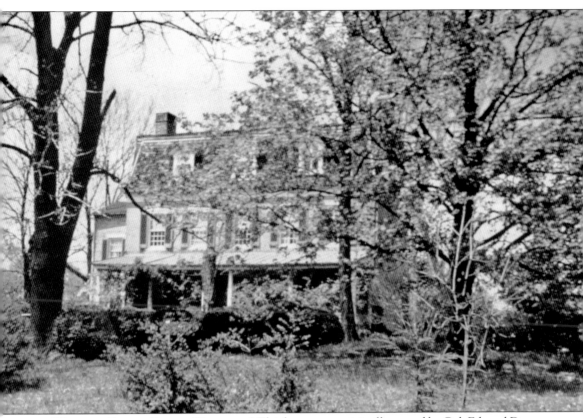

WINDSOR FARM—BURIED TREASURE? This house was originally owned by Col. Edward Dorsey, who, in 1701, built a two-story framed house. In 1793, it was substantially enlarged. In 1802, the property was sold to Jean deRoyer Champayne, a French émigré who sold his fleet of French merchant ships to avoid confiscation during the French Revolution and fled to the United States. Legend says that he and a manservant buried $50,000 to $100,000 in gold on the property. Champayne died, and the servant, on his deathbed, told the widow about the buried treasure, but not its exact location. Madame Champayne never found her husband's gold. In 1852, Col. William Devere purchased the property. The estate's final owner was Devere's granddaughter, Janet Ball. Many have searched, but none have found the buried gold. Some say that Champayne himself can be seen, once a year on the night of a full August moon, looking for his gold. Devere Road, once the main entrance to the farm, is all that remains of Windsor Farm. The house was razed in the 1960s, and Westchester Elementary School was built on the back of the property. (Courtesy of the Catonsville Room.)

Three

MAIN STREET
AND BEYOND

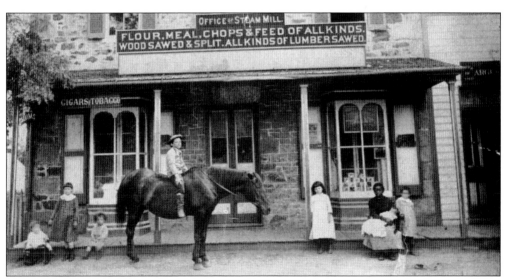

ALBERT SMITH'S OFFICE AND HOME—701 FREDERICK ROAD, C. 1881. Built in 1855, Mr. Smith had his office of the Smith Steam Mill in the front rooms of his home. Through the years, it has had its facade drastically altered and currently houses Dixon Signs. (Courtesy of the Catonsville Room.)

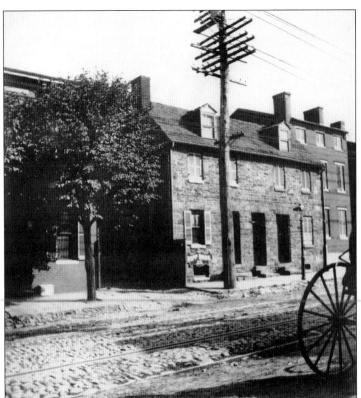

FREDERICK ROAD, 432-434, C. 1905. This photograph shows old stone houses remaining from the early days of Frederick Road. Bopp Brothers Ice Company was occupying the house in 1905. (Courtesy of the Enoch Pratt Free Library.)

FREDERICK ROAD, 2323-2325, C. 1914. Notice the unusual timber and brick construction here. (Courtesy of the Enoch Pratt Free Library.)

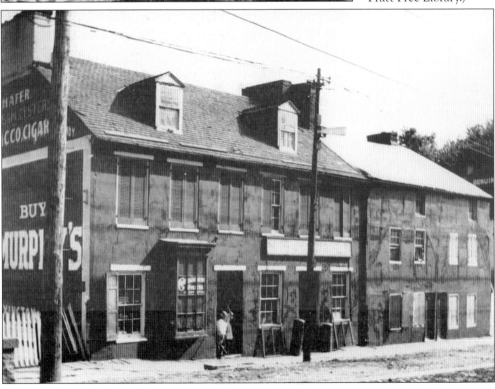

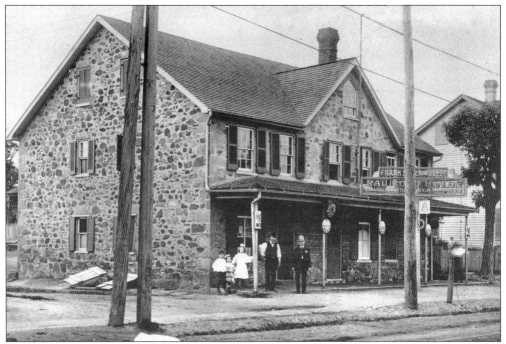

THE RAILROAD HOTEL, C. 1900. The hotel was located at Frederick Road and Egges Lane. It stood opposite the Catonsville Short Line Terminus. The hotel was sold in 1922 and razed to make room for the new Catonsville firehouse, previously located at 22 Bloomsbury Avenue. (Courtesy of the Catonsville Room.)

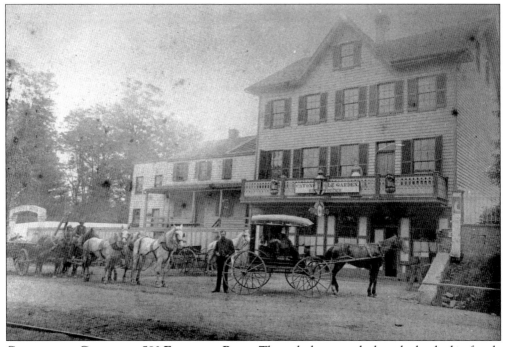

CATONSVILLE GARDENS—583 FREDERICK ROAD. Through the years, the hostelry has had its facade drastically altered and current houses G. L. Shacks Grill. (Courtesy of the Catonsville Room.)

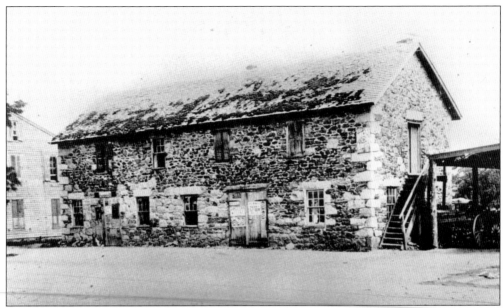

REMUS ADAMS'S BLACKSMITH SHOP. Catonsville has been the home for numerous African American families, both during and after the slavery years. Remus Adams, an African American man, ran a successful business during slavery. He owned a blacksmith shop at the intersection of Frederick Road and Bloomsbury Avenue. In 1909, the stone shop was razed, and the Catonsville High School, now the elementary school, was built. (Courtesy of the Catonsville Room.)

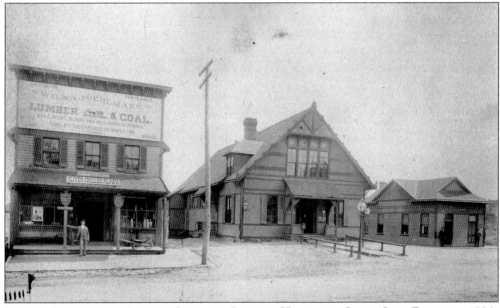

WILSON & POEHLMAN LUMBER COMPANY, LIBRARY HALL, AND SHORT LINE DEPOT, C. 1890. These three businesses were located on the south side of the 700 block of Frederick Road. From left to right are Wilson & Poehlman's Lumber and Coal Dealers; Library Hall, used for public meetings, social events, and theatrical productions (which housed the post office at that time, and later the First National Bank); and the Catonsville Short Line Railroad Depot. By 1884, the Baltimore-to-Catonsville line was complete. (Courtesy of the Catonsville Room.)

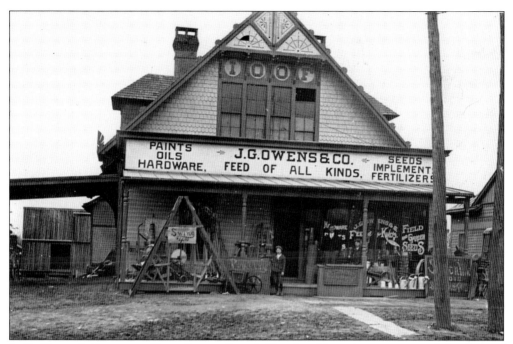

J. G. Owens's Seed and Feed Store. Josuah Goucher Owens's store occupied the front of Library Hall, selling "feed of all kinds" and "field and green seeds." The double garden swing on the left could be purchased for $4. Notice the "IOOF" letters above the second-floor windows. It housed the Independent Order of Odd Fellows (IOOF), which later move to Ingleside Avenue. (Courtesy of the Catonsville Room.)

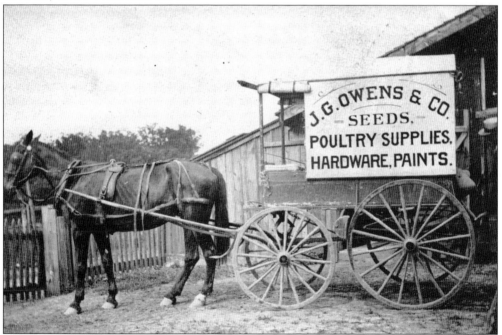

Delivery Wagon of J. G. Owens Feed Store, late 19th Century. J. G. Owens were providers of seeds, poultry supplies, hardware, and paints. (Courtesy of the Catonsville Room.)

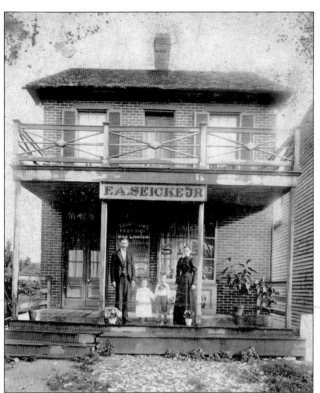

F. A. Seicke Jr., 1895—715 Frederick Road. This building housed the telegraph office in the 1880s. According to the signage, Seicke provided "Telephones, Electric, Gas Lighting, Call Bells, Burglar Alarms, Door Bells and Sign Painting." The building was later used as a doctor's office and was torn down in the 1950s. In 1970, the Catonsville office of the Social Security Administration was built on this location. (Courtesy of the Catonsville Room.)

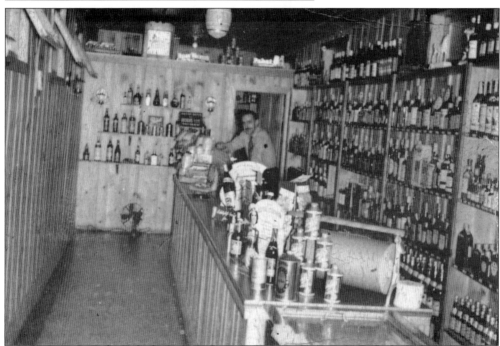

Catonsville Liquor Store, June 22, 1939. Pictured here is proprietor Bill Lawrence. The store was located at 900 Frederick Road, the current location of R. C. Rodger's Gourmet Deli & Liquors. (Courtesy of Trip Riley.)

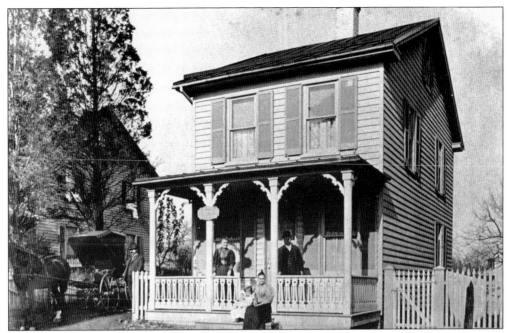

DR. CHARLES MATTFELDT, C. 1885—908 FREDERICK ROAD. This was the first office and home of Dr. Mattfeldt. He would later move a few blocks down the street. Pictured here are Lem Schwinesberg (by carriage); Dr. Mattfeldt and his wife Wilhemina Schromsberg Mattfeldt (on porch); and a child and a woman, possibly Schwinesbergs. The law firm of McFarland & Masters, L.L.P., is the building's current resident. (Courtesy of the Catonsville Room.)

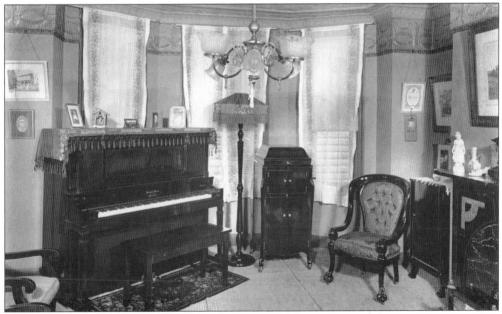

DR. CHARLES MATTFELDT'S FRONT PARLOR. Seen here is the front parlor of Dr. Mattfeldt's home in the 700 block of Frederick Road. Note the photograph hanging on the wall to the left of the Haines Brothers piano. It is a photograph of the location shown above, of Dr. Mattfeldt's first home and office on Frederick Road. (Courtesy of the Catonsville Room.)

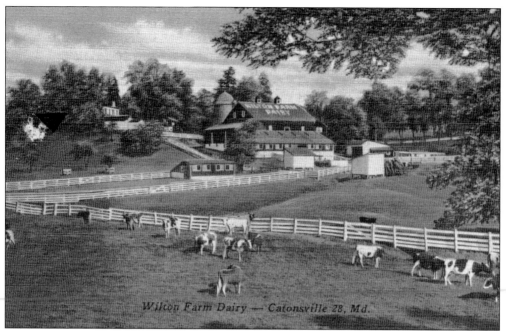

THE WILTON FARM DAIRY. This postcard advertisement reads, "Originated on this farm in 1880. Located at Wilkens Avenue and Maiden Choice Lane in Catonsville, MD, it is one of the most attractive dairy farms in MD—compromising 125 acres. The main office and plant is located at Frederick Ave., and Longwood St. Baltimore, 23, MD." (Courtesy of Trip Riley.)

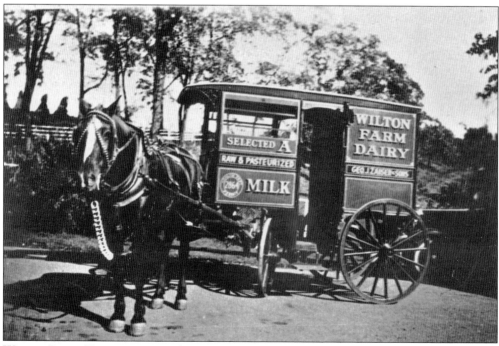

WILTON DAIRY TRUCK, C. 1933. The signage on the truck reads, "Selected A—Raw & Pasteurized Milk—Geo. J. Zaiser & Sons." (Courtesy of the Catonsville Room.)

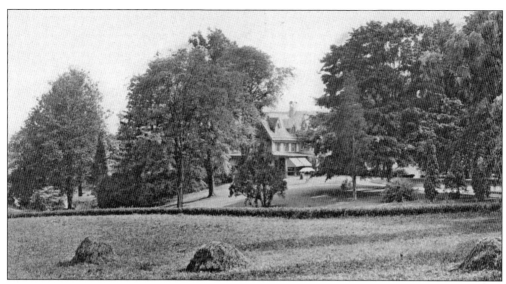

ELLERSLIE FARMS, C. 1919. The farm began in 1857 when the owner, Anthony Kennedy, purchased a Jersey cow named Alice Gray. Ellerslie was known for its purebred Jersey line. Kennedy died in 1894. His great-grandson, C. Hughes Manly, took over managing the farm. Manly died in 1918 at the National Dairy Show of Columbus. The farm was located at 2501 Frederick Road and is currently home to the Patapsco Horse Center. (Courtesy of the author's collection.)

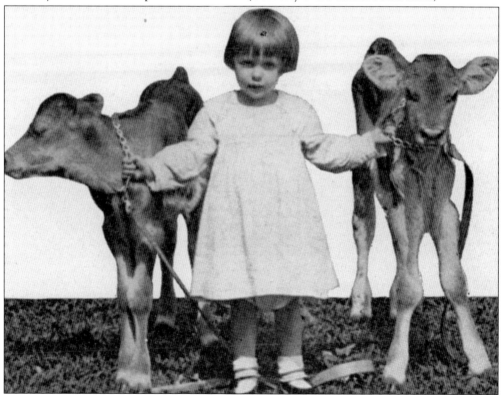

ELLERSLIE FARMS, C. 1919. Their motto was "Every producer a show cow, and every show cow a producer." (Courtesy of the author's collection.)

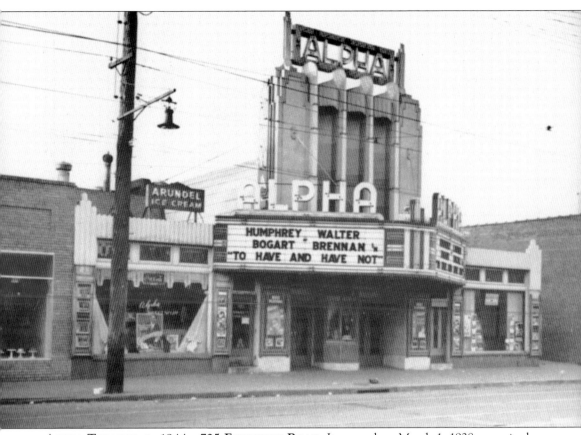

ALPHA THEATRE, C. 1944—725 FREDERICK ROAD. It opened on March 1, 1928, as a single-screen theater seating over 500 people. The Alpha closed in the 1960s. The building has been altered and used as various stores, but a check in the rear of the block reveals the theater, with the back twice as long as the other buildings. It currently houses the Catonsville Custom Framing & Fine Art store. (Courtesy of the Catonsville Room.)

ALPHA THEATRE OPENING PROGRAM, MARCH 1, 1928. Listed in the program for the first week are the following: *Sorrell and Son*, March 1-2; *In Old Kentucky*, March 3; *The Student Prince in Heidelberg* (the spectacular operetta), March 5-6; *Chang*, March 7; *The Bugle Call* (Jackie Coogan in a great picture), March 8; *The Big Parade*, starring John Gilbert with Renee Adoree, March 9–10. Programs were mailed weekly and handed out at the door. (Courtesy of the Catonsville Room.)

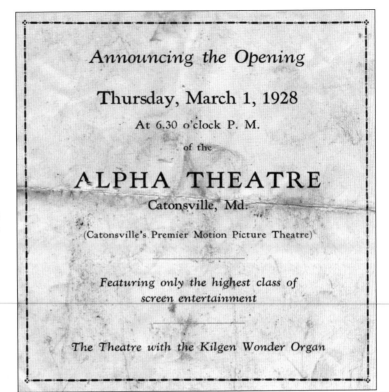

Announcing the Opening

Thursday, March 1, 1928

At 6.30 o'clock P. M.

of the

ALPHA THEATRE

Catonsville, Md.

(Catonsville's Premier Motion Picture Theatre)

Featuring only the highest class of screen entertainment

The Theatre with the Kilgen Wonder Organ

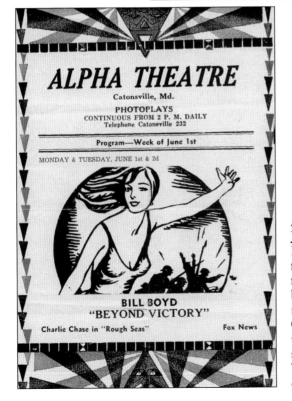

ALPHA THEATRE PROGRAM, WEEK OF JUNE 1, 1931. The theater was featuring Bill Boyd in *Beyond Victory*, a movie about four battle-weary American soldiers under fire who reflect on the women they left behind. Also featured that week was a movie short, *Rough Seas*, starring Charlie Chase, about an American soldier on his way home following World War I who smuggles his French sweetheart (Thelma Todd) aboard ship and gets into all kinds of trouble. (Courtesy of James Vidmar.)

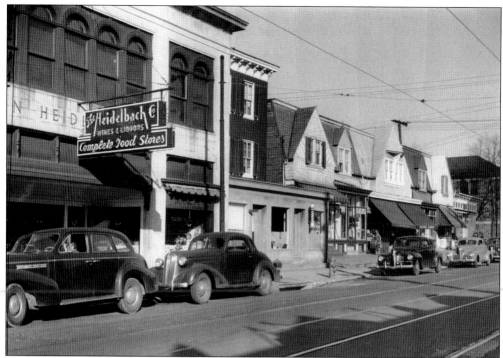

THE HEIDELBACH COMPANY, C. 1945. The Heidelbach's first grocery store was opened in 1882 and was located at 918 Frederick Road. In 1925, they built and moved to the location pictured here at 720 Frederick Road. They were a grocery store chain of two, with the other store being located in Roland Park. The stores closed in 1965. Plymouth Wallpapers currently occupies the building. (Courtesy of the Catonsville Room.)

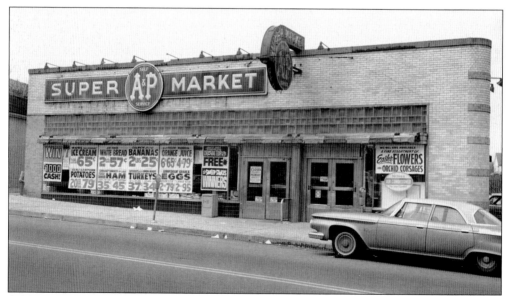

A&P SUPERMARKET, MARCH 1967. Located on the site of the former Raab residence, the A&P was located in the 900 block of Frederick on the north side from the 1930s to the 1950s. (Courtesy of the Catonsville Room.)

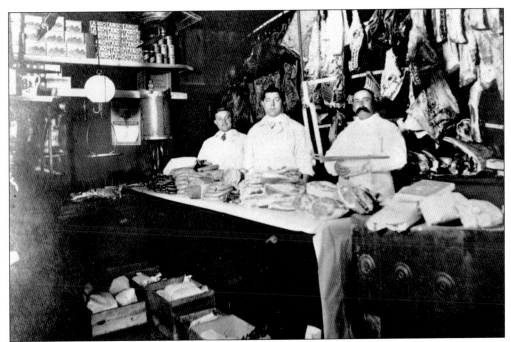

WHITNEY-GARDNER BUTCHER SHOP. This shop was located in the 700 block Frederick Road. Pictured here from left to right are Toddie Whitney, Louis Poehlmann, and Mr. Gardner. (Courtesy of the Catonsville Room.)

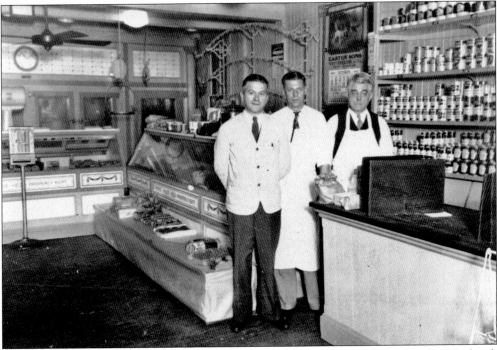

POEHLMANN GROCERY & MEATS, C. 1949. This store was located in the 800 block of Frederick Road. Pictured here, from left to right, are Norman, Luther, and Louis Poehlmann. (Courtesy of the Catonsville Room.)

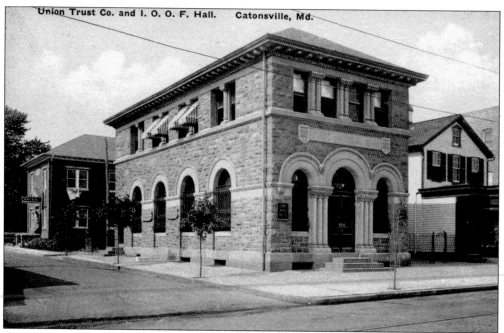

UNION TRUST COMPANY AND IOOF HALL POSTCARD. The bank was built in 1922. The IOOF Hall, built in 1909, can be seen behind the bank. Currently, Colquitt Design and Alterego are located in the old bank building. (Courtesy of William Hollifield.)

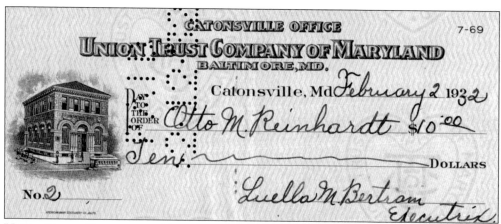

UNION TRUST COMPANY OF MARYLAND CHECK, FEBRUARY 2, 1932. This check was made payable to Otto M. Reinhardt in the amount of $10 and signed by Luella M. Bertram, executrix. Note the fine detail in the artwork of the bank building on the check. It was common for banks to include such drawings on their checks at that time. (Courtesy of William Hollifield.)

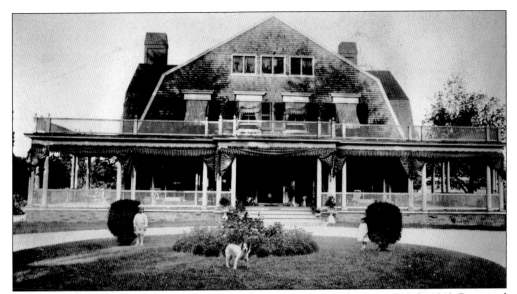

GLYNN TAFF, HOME OF REV. A. OPITZ, C. 1918. This home was built in 1903. In 1918, Reverend Opitz purchased the house and opened a home for aged and invalids. Today it is still an assisted-living facility operating as Glynn Taff Assisted Living, and it is located at 5741 Edmondson Avenue. (Courtesy of the Catonsville Room.)

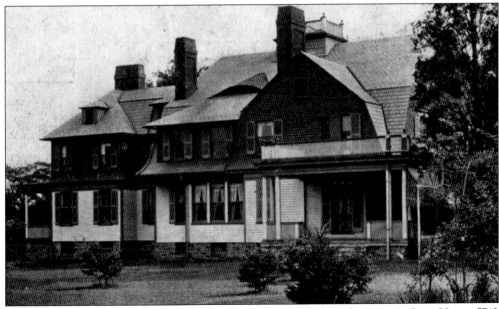

REV. A. OPITZ HOME POSTCARD. The description on the back reads, "Rev. A. Opitz Home, 5743 Edmondson Ave., Nunnery lane, A private home for aged and invalids, est. 1918." (Courtesy of William Hollifield.)

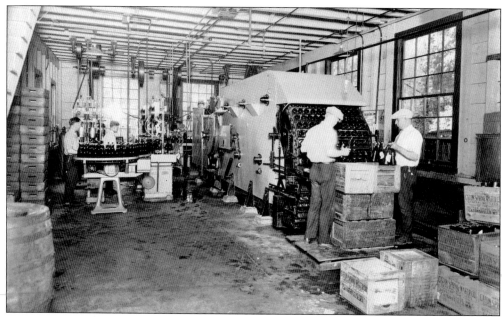

CATON SPRING WATER COMPANY BOTTLING ROOM, C. 1926. The room is located on the site of the Caton Water Company, started by Victor Bloede to supply water to the Eden Terrace development in the 1880s. Utilizing the same springs, the Caton Spring Water Company began in 1903. They produced carbonated beverages, such as their own brand of ginger ale. Other flavors included Caton Kola, sarsaparilla, and lemon, chocolate, grape, and strawberry sodas. (Courtesy of the Catonsville Room.)

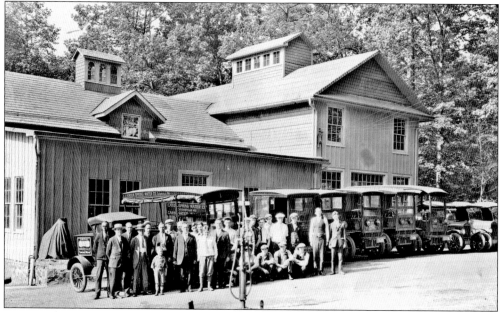

CATON SPRING WATER COMPANY DELIVERY TRUCKS, MAY 30, 1926. The company advertised that "Carbonation, Doctors tell us, has a decided dietic value. Carbonated Gas is a digestive stimulant. That's why hospitals serve Caton Ginger Ale regularly." The company was acquired by 7-Up in 1937. (Courtesy of the Catonsville Room.)

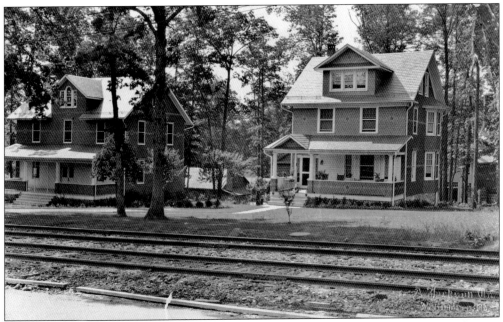

ENTRANCE TO THE CATONSVILLE WATER COMPANY, 6159 EDMONDSON AVENUE. The two asbestos-shingled houses seen here flank either side of the drive to the water company. The trolley-car tracks in front transported workers daily. These homes are still recognizable today and have maintained the patterns in the shingle work. The 1948 7-Up building still stands and serves as the Catonsville Transmission & Engine Repair shop. (Courtesy of the Catonsville Room.)

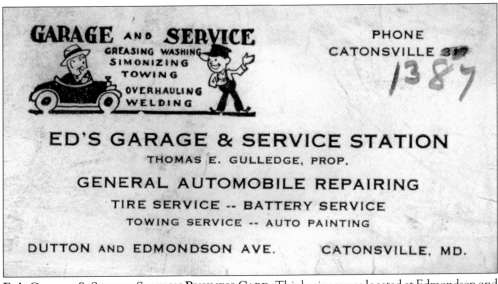

ED'S GARAGE & SERVICE STATION BUSINESS CARD. This business was located at Edmondson and Dutton Avenues, and Thomas E. Gulledge was the proprietor. (Courtesy of William Hollifield.)

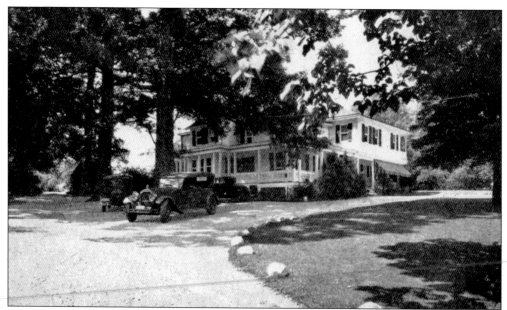

FIVE OAKS LODGE POSTCARD, 1920s. This was originally a private home, known as the Five Oaks estate, built in 1850. The postcard reads, "Five Oaks Lodge, Eight Miles West of Baltimore, Maryland, on the National Highway, between Catonsville and Ellicott City." In the mid-1920s, the Rogers family, owners at the time, began offering afternoon tea and light fare in the parlors and on the gracious porch. The Candle Light Inn continues the tradition today. (Courtesy of the author's collection.)

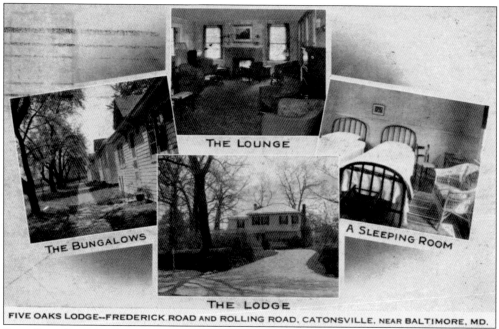

THE LOUNGE

THE BUNGALOWS

A SLEEPING ROOM

THE LODGE

FIVE OAKS LODGE—FREDERICK ROAD AND ROLLING ROAD, CATONSVILLE, NEAR BALTIMORE, MD.

FIVE OAKS LODGE POSTCARD—POSTMARKED 1930. Ten or twelve little cottages were built behind the house to accommodate people traveling between Baltimore and Washington. (Courtesy of William Hollifield.)

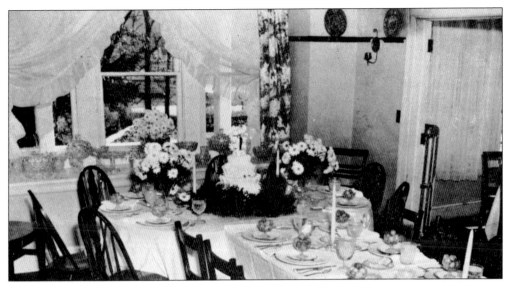

ANNA MAY CALK'S CANDLE LIGHT LODGE POSTCARD, POSTMARKED 1949. In the early 1940s, the house was purchased by Anna May Calk, who served a bountiful spread of traditional Maryland food for over 20 years. Anna May retired in the early 1960s and sold the inn to Charles and Ginny Dukehart, who maintained the inn for close to 15 years, until an electrical fire destroyed the porch and damaged the small adjoining dining room. In 1979, the Lombardini family repaired and reopened the inn. (Courtesy of William Hollifield.)

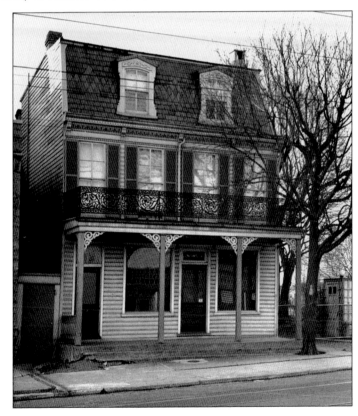

PETZOLD'S SALOON—905 FREDERICK ROAD. This building was razed to make room for Salem Evangelical Lutheran Church's expansion. (Courtesy of the Catonsville Room.)

81

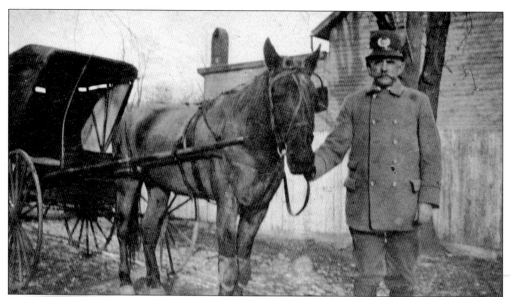

G. G. ROBINSON, POSTMAN. Robinson delivered mail in Catonsville from 1890 to about 1925. (Courtesy of the Catonsville Room.)

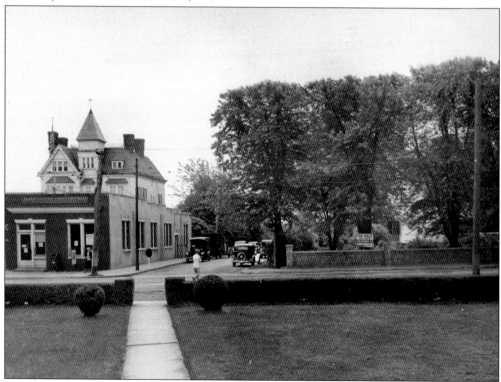

CATONSVILLE POST OFFICE, 1922–1933. The post office was located at 927 Frederick Road. The property to the right of the post office, on which the "For Sale" sign can be seen, was the Jobson residence (see page 4). The post office razed the home and built the current post office. Take note of the mansion behind the post office. It served as an apartment building at the time and was later torn down. (Courtesy of the Enoch Pratt Free Library.)

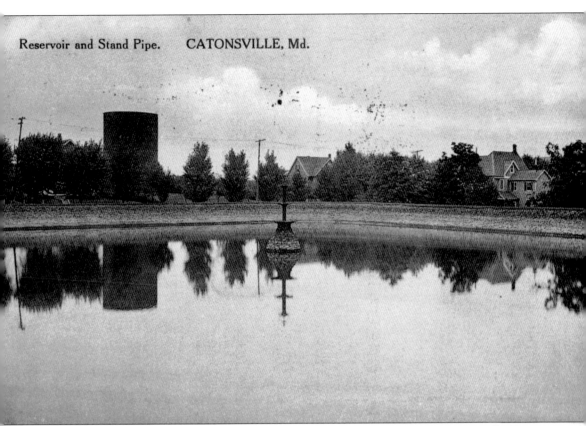

Reservoir and Stand Pipe.   CATONSVILLE, Md.

RESERVOIR AND STAND PIPE POSTCARD, POSTMARKED 1916. In 1894, the Catonsville Water Company constructed a reservoir with a capacity of six million gallons on the west side of Melvin Avenue, in the center of the block, and took down the standpipes. Some residents complained that the reservoir would have a negative impact on their neighborhood, but the water company countered, "The reservoir, if the present plans are to be carried out, will appear as a beautiful lake surrounded with terrace paths and sodded plats. It will be a beautiful ornament to the avenue." When completed, it was enclosed by an iron fence and had a fountain in the center. In addition to the reservoir, which was constructed by J. P. Morgan of Baltimore, a steel water tank was erected on the east side of Melvin Avenue. In very little time, the reservoir began to leak on account of several muskrat holes and had to be re-puddled (made watertight) with clay. In 1937, the current water tower was constructed to replace the reservoir. The water tower is a domed structure built of a buff brick with limestone Art Deco trimmings. (Courtesy of William Hollifield.)

OLIVIA VORDEMBERGE

519 Hilton Ave. Catonsville, Md.

☎ CAtonsville 9 3 4 - R

(Will Come To Your Home By Appointment)

Finger Wave 50c.　　Marcel Wave (on top only) 50c

Marcel Wave (underneath) 75c

FACIALS: Plain 50c

Bleach,　Egg $1.25　Meal $1.00　Lemon $1.50

Blackhead Treatment 75c To RemoveHair From Face 50c

Eye Arch without cream 35c Eye Arch Hoyt's Painless 50c

Manicure 40c Hot Oil Treatment (without Shampoo) 40c

Hot Oil Treatment(with vibrator) 50c Hot Oil Treatment

(with shampoo) 75c　　Iodine Peel For Dandruff 50c

Tar Treatment 75c Scalp Treatment (with vibrator) 50c

(without vibrator) 40c　　Hair Cut 25c

Shampoo Short 25c　Long 50c　　Thinning 35c

"Parker Herbeck's" for bald spots, also falling hair $1.50

"Roux" Shampoo and Tint any shade $1.50

OLIVIA VORDEMBERGE, BEAUTICIAN. This advertisement for Olivia Vordemberge, who lived at 519 Hilton Avenue sometime after 1921, states that she would come to your home. The "Marcel Wave" offered was popular in the mid-1920s so that smaller hats, such as a cloche, could be worn. (Courtesy of William Hollifield.)

84

Four

HALLOWED HALLS OF LEARNING

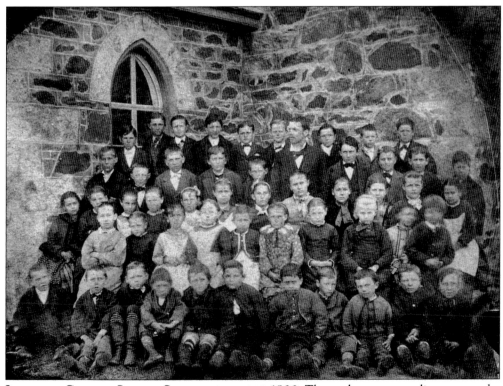

INGLESIDE GERMAN SCHOOL STUDENTS, BEFORE 1900. The students are standing next to the Old Salem Lutheran Church on Ingleside Avenue. (Courtesy of the Catonsville Room.)

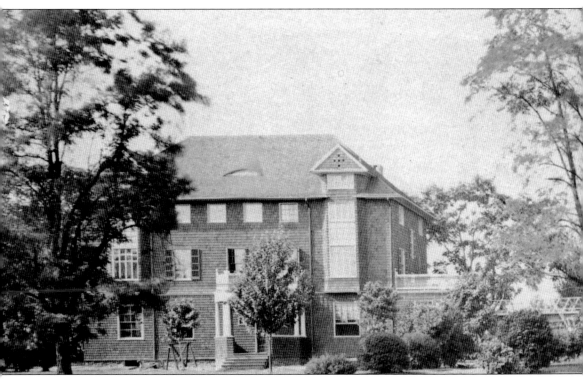

St. Timothy's School for Girls, 1891. St. Timothy's School for Girls began on Fusting Avenue in 1882. In the 1880s, several frame buildings were erected on the location of the no-longer-existent St. Timothy's Hall, and the girls' school moved there. It was a very exclusive school established by Misses Sallie and Polly Carter. In 1952, the school sold the property to St. Timothy's Church and moved to Stevenson, Maryland. The buildings were razed in 1967. On June 9, 1909, Mark Twain

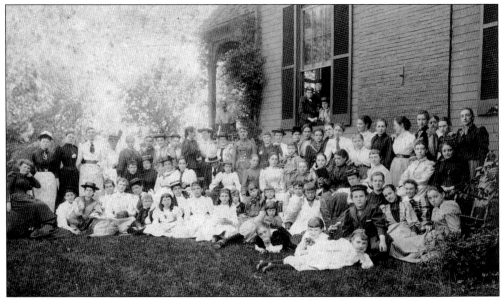

St. Timothy's School for Girls, 1891–1892. Note the boys shown in the photograph of the all-girls school. (Courtesy of the Catonsville Room.)

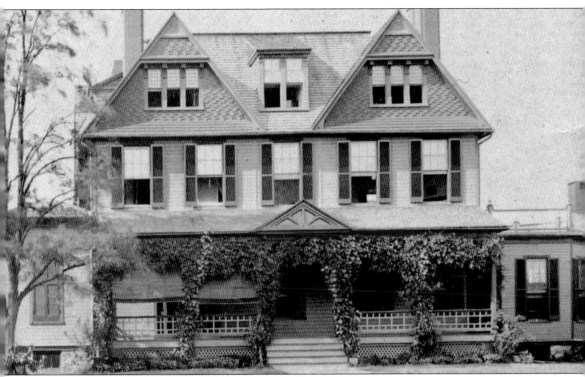

gave his last public address at the school. His advice to the girls was, "First, girls, don't smoke to excess. I am seventy-three and a half years old, and have been smoking seventy-three of them. But I never smoke to excess—that is, I smoke in moderation, only one cigar at a time. Second, don't drink to excess. Third, don't marry to excess." (Courtesy of the Catonsville Room.)

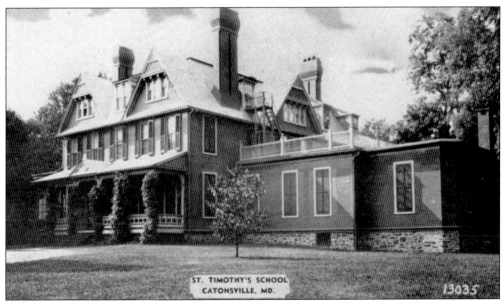

ST. TIMOTHY'S SCHOOL POSTCARD. This building was razed in 1967. (Courtesy of William Hollifield.)

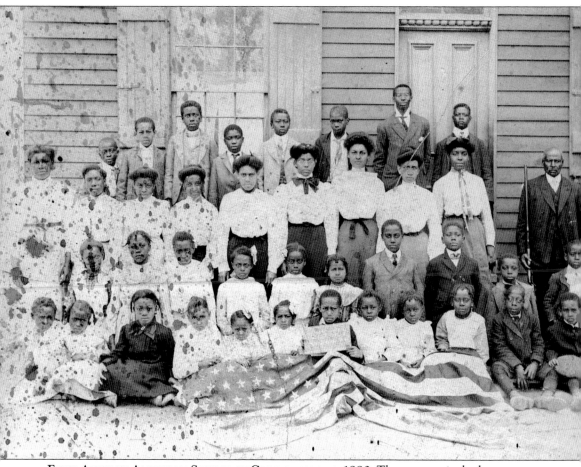

FIRST AFRICAN AMERICAN SCHOOL IN CATONSVILLE, C. 1880. The community had a one-room school for African American children that was built shortly after the end of slavery in 1868. That building was torn down to the foundation and the Full Gospel Tabernacle Baptist Church was built on the foundation. In the very early days, the African American children were educated only to the sixth grade. In 1923, a larger school was built on Wesley Avenue for educating African American students (Banneker School, P. S. #21) that went through the 11th grade. In 1951, 12 full years of education were offered. The church is located at 100 Winters Lane. (Courtesy of the Catonsville Room.)

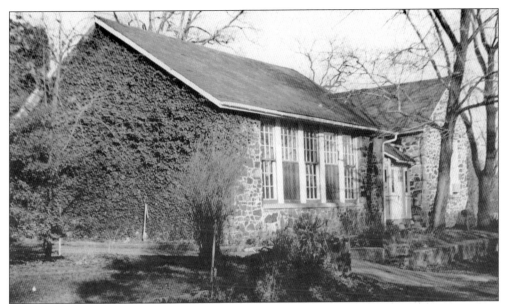

JOHNNYCAKE SCHOOL HOUSE. The school was located near North Rolling Road and possibly built about 1820 as a one-room school with the addition on the right being added in 1900. It was heated with a small stove, and the children wrote on slates in the early years. The school was converted into a residence in 1940. The former school was razed in 1964 for the construction of I-70N. (Courtesy of the Catonsville Room.)

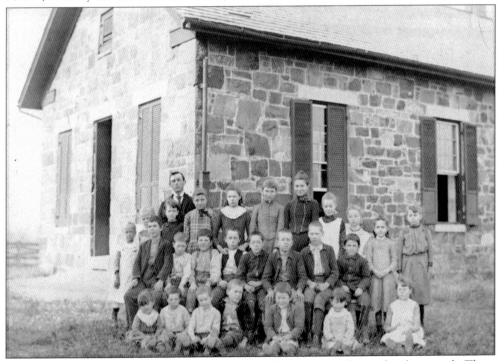

JOHNNYCAKE SCHOOL HOUSE STUDENTS. J. Albert Kalb is the teacher in the photograph. There was no running water or indoor plumbing in the school. Drinking water was brought from a well outside. (Courtesy of the Catonsville Room.)

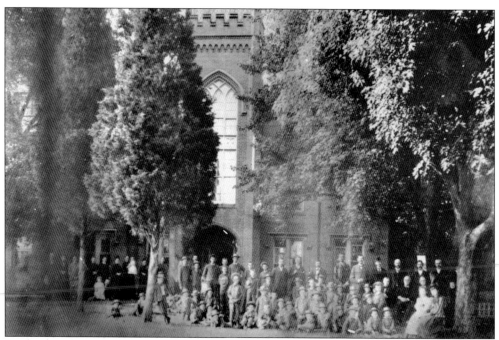

BOYS MANUAL LABOR SCHOOL FOR INDIGENT BOYS, C. 1890. Also known as the Arbutus Farm School, it was started in 1840. In 1842, there were 26 inmates in the frame house. The large stone building pictured was built in 1860. In 1916, it burned from boys spitting kerosene oil and lighting it with a match to look as if they were breathing fire. The University of Maryland, Baltimore County (UMBC) now owns the land. (Courtesy of the Catonsville Room.)

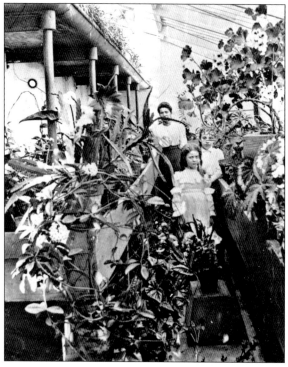

MANUAL LABOR SCHOOL GREENHOUSE, C. 1884. Hester Stabler, wife of the superintendent, Edmund Stabler, ran the greenhouse with her daughters, Rebecca and Lillian. The carnations and lovely double, sweet-scented violets were always in demand. This photograph was taken by Emily Spencer Hayden. (Courtesy of the Catonsville Room.)

OVERLEA COLLEGE, BUILT 1860—108 DELREY AVENUE. Rev. Dr. George W. Eberling, pastor of Salem Lutheran Church, built the house for use as his home and the school. It was designed to resemble a castle on the Rhine in Germany, from which the reverend had emigrated in 1853. The first two floors were used as the family quarters, with the third floor as the dormitory for the schoolboys. The school closed in 1895. (Courtesy of the Catonsville Room.)

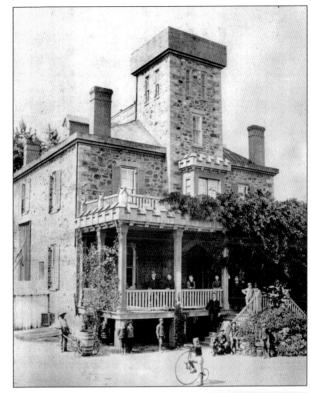

OVERLEA COLLEGE. Pictured in the foreground are Rev. Dr. George W. Eberling and his wife, Maria Keidel Eberling. Delrey Avenue now runs along what was the driveway from Edmondson Avenue to the 12-acre property. The home still stands on 1.3 acres and is a private residence. (Courtesy of the Catonsville Room.)

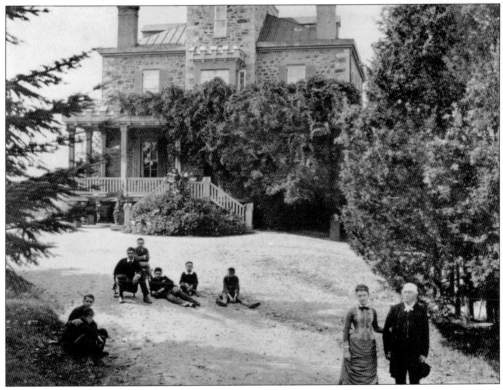

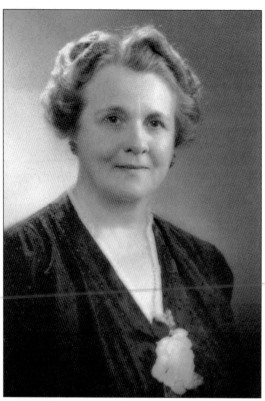

MARY LOUISE KEMP (1887–1975) IN 1937. She was the owner and headmistress at the Crosby School from 1922 until she closed it in 1967. The school was founded in 1895 by Ethel Crosby in her home at 20 North Beaumont Avenue. (Courtesy of the Catonsville Room.)

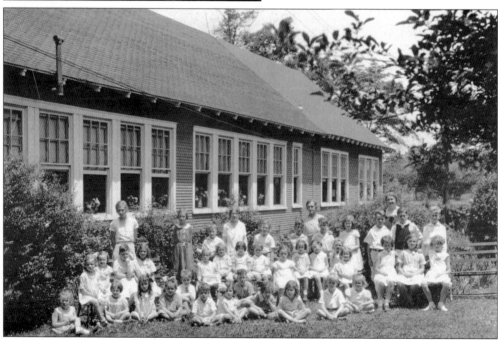

CROSBY SCHOOL HOUSE. A schoolroom was built in 1914 and later enlarged in 1929. It burned down on April 8, 1976, during a two-alarm fire. The Kemp-Crosby house still stands at 20 North Beaumont Avenue as a private residence. (Courtesy of the Catonsville Room.)

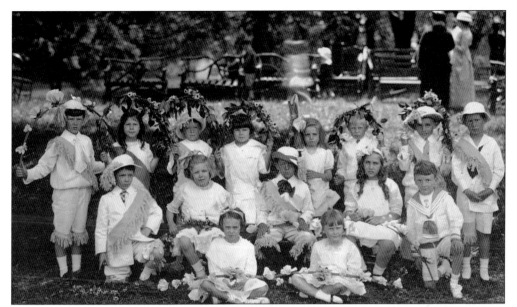

CROSBY SCHOOL, 1914. The following is from the poem "Evangeline" by Henry Wadsworth Longfellow: "Crowned with Asphodel flowers that are wet with dews of Nepenthe." He was Miss Crosby's favorite poet. Pictured from left to right are the following: (first row) Florence Kimberly and Frances Gieske; (second row) Harry Yardley, Elizabeth Miller, George Washington Perine, Rachel Gundry, and George Knipp; (third row) Henry Keidel, Elizabeth Schermerhorn, unidentified, Irmagarde Stude, Alice Schnibbe, Bobby Womble, Alexander Crosby, and Bill McMillan. (Courtesy of the Catonsville Room.)

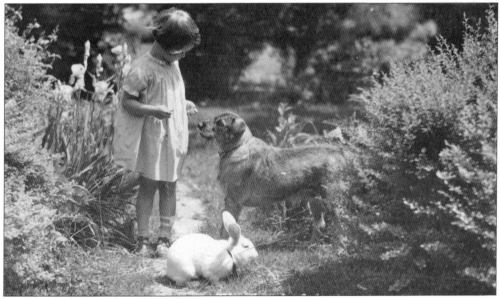

THE CROSBY SCHOOL MASCOTS POSTCARD, C. 1940. Shown here is the Crosby mascot, Lucky the dog, with Peter Cottontail and Laura Jane Freund. Lucky was a schnauzer that wandered into the school on a rainy, foggy morning in March 1936. He shook hands, sat up, begged, and then lay on the floor with his jaws on his paws and continued to be the best "student" for eight years. He died in June 1945 of a heart ailment. (Courtesy of the Catonsville Room.)

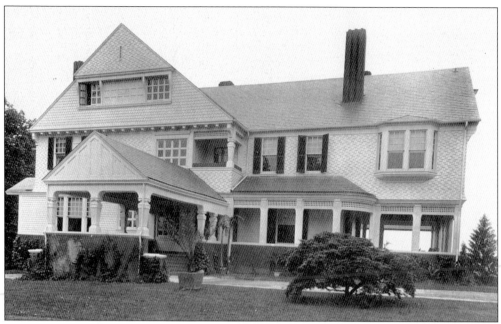

THE ROBERTS-BEACH SCHOOL FOR GIRLS, C. 1911. The school was located in a large frame house known as Searsleighs, built in 1898 as a home by Maj. John S. Gibbs. He was a member of the board of managers at Spring Grove Hospital in 1919. The school was founded in 1920 by Lucy George Roberts, Ph.D., and Sarah Morehouse Beach, Ph.D. Both women were graduates of Mount Holyoke and wanted to start a preparatory school for their alma mater. There were only 12 students the first year. (Courtesy of the Catonsville Room.)

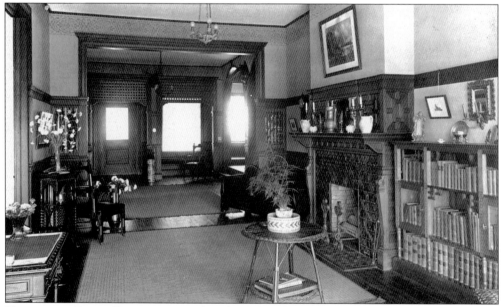

KENWOOD—FRONT HALL, C. 1911. The school closed in 1940 after a decline in enrollment that started during the Depression. In 1953, the house had been subdivided into residential apartments. It accidentally caught fire and burned down. The Western School of Technology, located at 100 Kenmore Avenue, sits on the property today. (Courtesy of the Catonsville Room.)

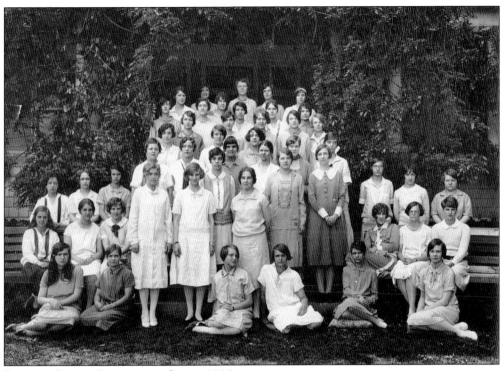

ROBERTS BEACH SCHOOL FOR GIRLS, 1920S.
Oddly, the back of this old photograph lists who is not in the photograph: "Elizabeth Daly (sp), Laura Nesbitt, and Carlota deBullet (52 girls in all)." The uniform was a skirt, any kind of middy blouse, thick cotton stockings, oxfords, and no jewelry. (Courtesy of the Catonsville Room.)

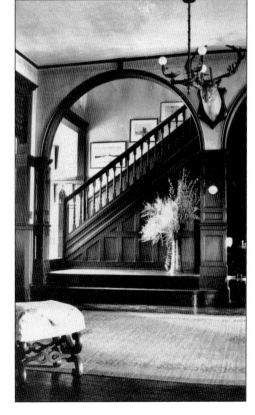

KENWOOD STAIRCASE, C. 1911. Two additional cottages, named Kencot and Kennex, respectively, were built on the property to house students and faculty. It was both a boarding school and a day school. Many Crosby School graduates attended. (Courtesy of the Catonsville Room.)

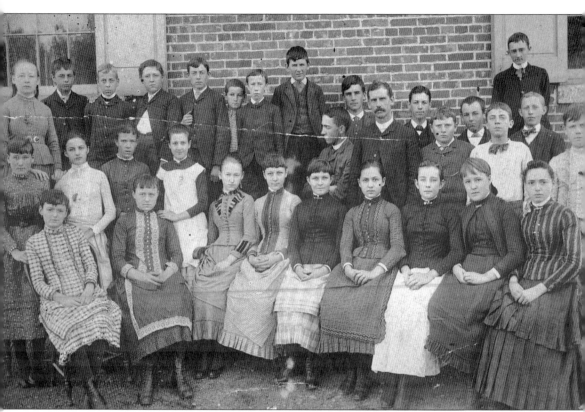

THE CATONSVILLE SCHOOL, C. 1881. The public school system began in Catonsville in a wooden building on the corner of Winters Lane and Melrose Avenue. The following members of the sixth and seventh grades are pictured from left to right: (first row) Maggie Meeth, Molhe Doyle, Julia W. Jones, Laura Platt, Ida Schotta, Olive Rose, Mami Fisher, Mary Watson, and Milly Reed; (second row) Katie Hensler, Camila Rentz (Whitney), Lena Meeth, Mary Kalb, Alfred Gundry, George Camalier, Edward G. Comegys (principal), Charles Kalb, Allan Towles, Albert Kalb, Arthur Coskery, Smith Horsey, John Reich, and Lillie Gerry; (third row) Edith H. Jones, Sam Gregg, Sam Helfrich, Will Gundry, Harry Donnelly, Jake Dauber, Joe McKeever, and Sam MacMillian. This building was improved from a wooden building in 1898. The building contained a small library and 12 classrooms. It was originally heated by coal, and students would complain that they had to open the windows in the winter to let out the smoke from the furnace. The building was sold to St. Mark Catholic Church, and a new school was erected on Frederick Road in 1910. (Courtesy of the Catonsville Room.)

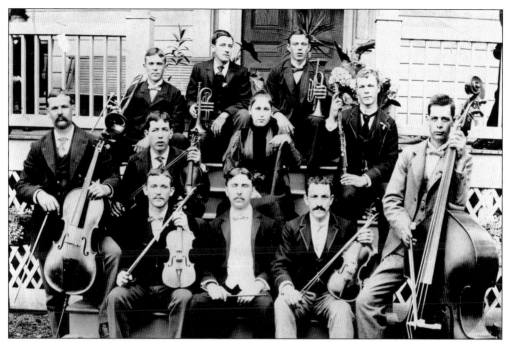

CATONSVILLE HIGH SCHOOL ORCHESTRA, 1880S. Pictured from left to right are as follows: (first row) two unidentified musicians and Jacob Bauman; (second row) Sim Dill, Katie Schaub, and ? Maisel; (third row); ? Maisel (third from left). All others are unidentified. (Courtesy of the Enoch Pratt Free Library.)

CATONSVILLE HIGH SCHOOL MEMBERS OF THE CLASS OF 1906. Amy Harris Walker is seated at left. (Courtesy of the Catonsville Room.)

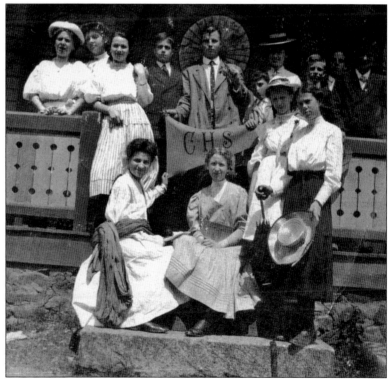

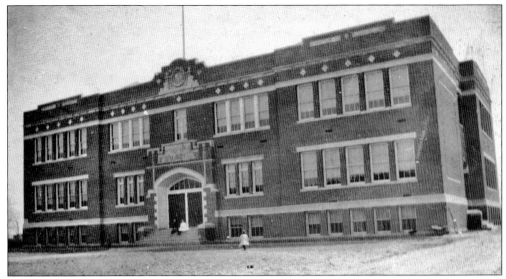

CATONSVILLE HIGH SCHOOL—FREDERICK ROAD, 1910. In 1910, Catonsville High School moved from its cramped quarters on Winters Lane to a $40,000 state-of-the-art building on Frederick Road, just east of Bloomsbury Avenue. The building contained a gymnasium, physics classroom, and outdoor fields, including a large track. The building currently houses Catonsville Elementary School. (Courtesy of the Catonsville Room.)

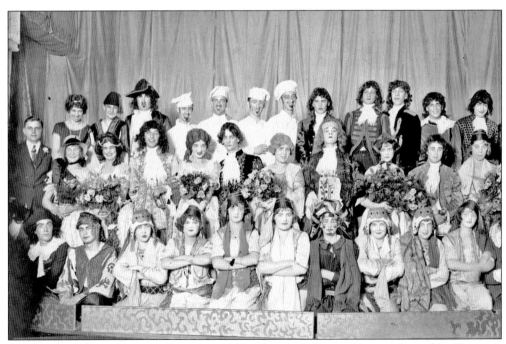

CATONSVILLE HIGH SCHOOL CLASS OF 1924. That year, the students performed *Le Bourgeois Gentilhomme* (The Would-be Gentleman), a *comédie-ballet* by Molière, first performed in France in 1670 for Louis XIV. (Courtesy of the Catonsville Room.)

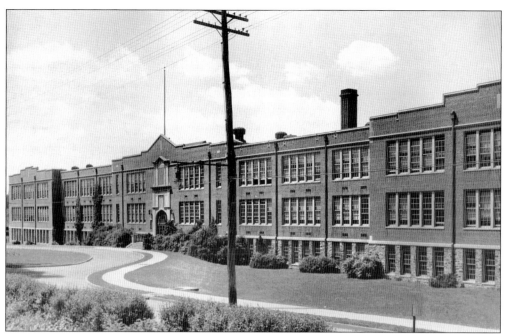

CATONSVILLE HIGH SCHOOL. In 1925, the high school moved to the Bloomsbury Avenue location after the board of education purchased the property from the Catonsville Country Club. Students were immediately impressed with the wide hallways and bright classrooms. (Courtesy of the Enoch Pratt Free Library.)

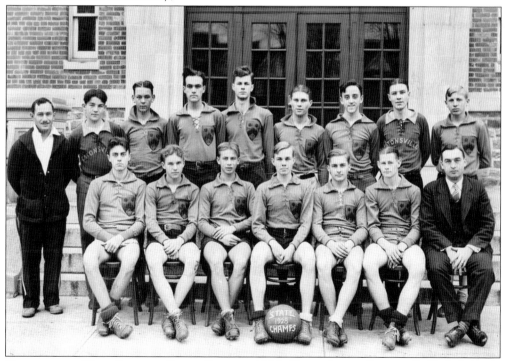

CATONSVILLE HIGH SCHOOL, STATE CHAMPS 1928. Shown here is Catonsville High School's 1928 state soccer champions. (Courtesy of the Catonsville Room.)

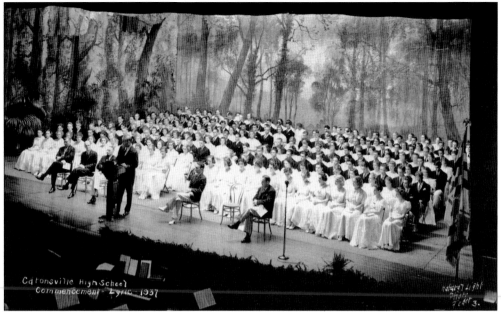

CATONSVILLE HIGH SCHOOL GRADUATION, 1937. In 1937, Catonsville High School began holding graduation ceremonies on stage at the Lyric Opera House in Baltimore. (Courtesy of Kitty Crider and Geraldine Hopwood.)

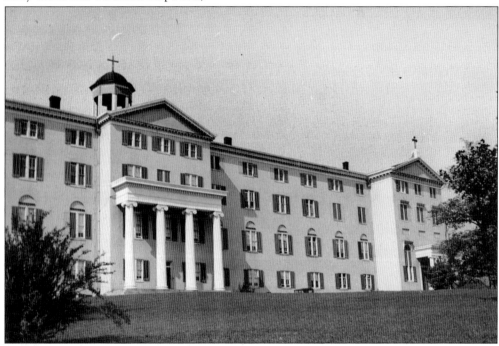

MOUNT DE SALES ACADEMY, OCTOBER 1936. Founded in 1852 as the Academy of the Visitation at Mount de Sales, the academy was open for the education of young women by Visitation nuns from Georgetown. The academy was the first institution in Baltimore County to offer education to young women of all denominations. It was placed on the National Register of Historical Places in 1986. (Courtesy of the Enoch Pratt Free Library.)

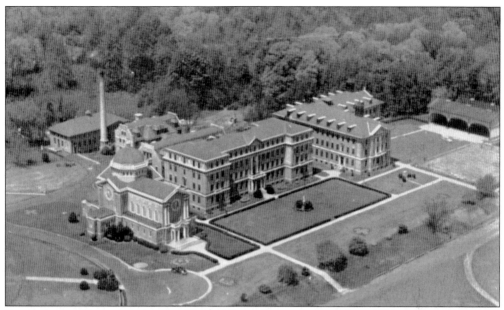

ST. CHARLES COLLEGE, AERIAL VIEW. The college relocated from Ellicott City after a fire in 1911 and was closed in 1977. The property, excepting Our Lady of the Angels Chapel and the Sulpician community cemetery, was sold and converted into the Charlestown Retirement Community. It was placed on the National Register of Historical Places in 1983. (Courtesy of William Hollifield.)

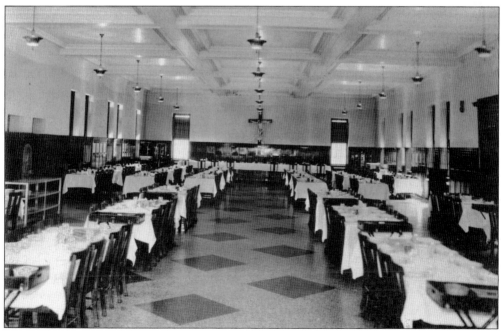

ST. CHARLES COLLEGE DINING HALL POSTCARD. This postcard was postmarked 1937. (Courtesy of William Hollifield.)

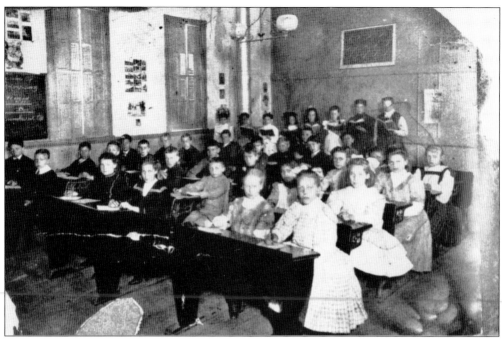

ST. MARK CATHOLIC SCHOOL CLASSROOM, C. 1910. St. Mark Catholic Church purchased the Catonsville Public School building in 1910. (Courtesy of the Catonsville Room.)

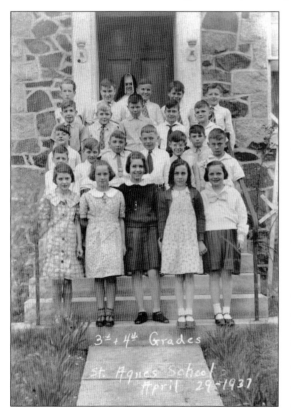

ST. AGNES SCHOOL THIRD AND FOURTH GRADES, APRIL 29, 1937. Pictured from left to right are as follows: (first row) Emma Waltman, Gertrude (Trudy) Brosenne, Mary Corey, Clarice Wood, and Rosemary Williamson; (second row) William Barrett, Clement Kuger, Edward Koener, Joe Moran, Edward Wolf, Paul Waltman, and Lawerence Williamson; (third row) Franklin Scharf, Joe Schene, Robert Bonsell, Bernard Hagarty, and Christopher Maddox; (fourth row) Edward Ghor, Paul Bryant, Sister Giletta, Earl Bryant, Charles Hispley, and George Anderton. The girl at left between the second and third rows is unidentified. (Courtesy of Catherine Anne "Muzzy" Fisher.)

Five

HOUSES OF WORSHIP

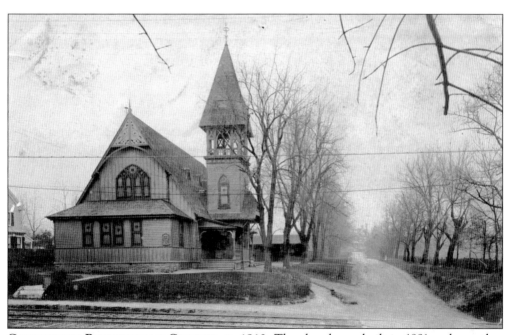

CATONSVILLE PRESBYTERIAN CHURCH, C. 1910. The church was built in 1881 and served as the house of worship for the Catonsville Presbyterian Church until 1922, when the congregation built and moved to the current location at Frederick Road and Beechwood Avenue. The church was sold to Christadelphian Chapel in 1922. The congregation still worships there. (Courtesy of William Hollifield.)

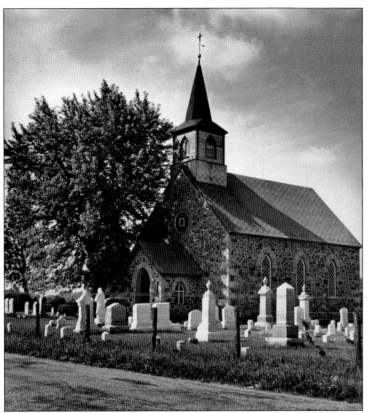

OLD SALEM LUTHERAN CHURCH, MAY 1937. The church was dedicated on Sunday, June 16, 1850. The next day, the following paragraph appeared in the Baltimore newspaper: "It is a very nice edifice, of Gothic style, surmounted by a pretty tower. The Rev. Benjamin Kurtz and the Rev. L. Van Bokkelen officiated during the day in German and English languages." It was placed on the National Register of Historical Places in 1977. (Courtesy of the Enoch Pratt Free Library.)

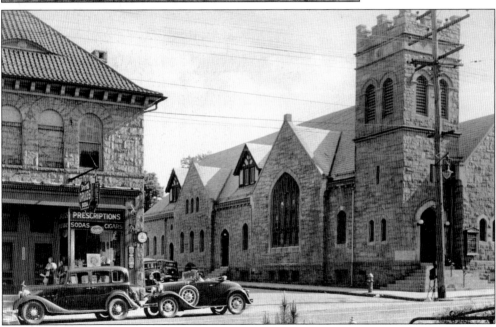

SALEM LUTHERAN CHURCH. By 1901, the congregation had outgrown its church, and it was decided to construct a new, larger one. The new church is located at Frederick Road and Newburg Avenue. (Courtesy of the Enoch Pratt Free Library.)

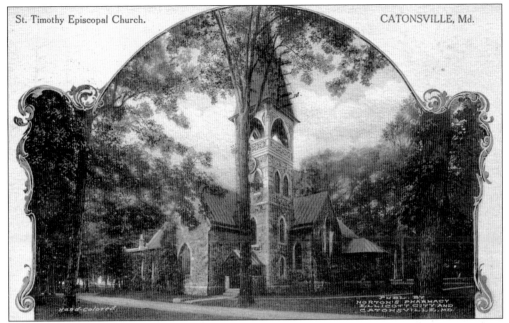

ST. TIMOTHY'S EPISCOPAL CHURCH, BUILT 1845. Catonsville's oldest church's congregation grew so rapidly that the original church was added onto in 1850. Additional expansions have been added since that time. The first rector was Rev. George F. Worthington. The church is depicted here on a postcard marked, "publ. By Norton's Pharmacy Ellicott City and Catonsville, MD." It was postmarked 1914. (Courtesy of William Hollifield.)

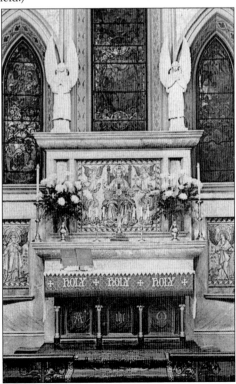

ST. TIMOTHY'S EPISCOPAL CHURCH ALTAR. Judge John Glenn of Hilton was the primary benefactor of the church and was honored in death by his burial on the church's front lawn. (Courtesy of William Hollifield.)

105

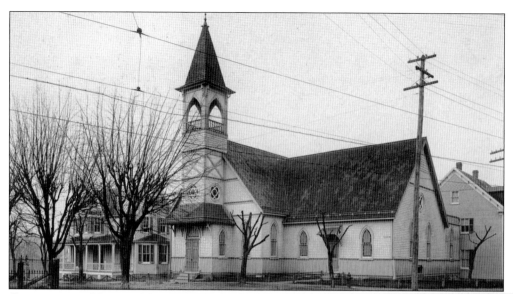

CATONSVILLE UNITED METHODIST CHURCH, C. 1910. The first Methodist minister in Catonsville began preaching in 1855 in private homes. By 1857, a stone church, called Providence Chapel, was erected on Bloomsbury Avenue on the current property of the Children's Home. The church pictured on this postcard was dedicated in 1887 on the corner of Frederick Road and Melvin Avenue. The parsonage, seen directly behind the church, was built in 1891. (Courtesy of William Hollifield.)

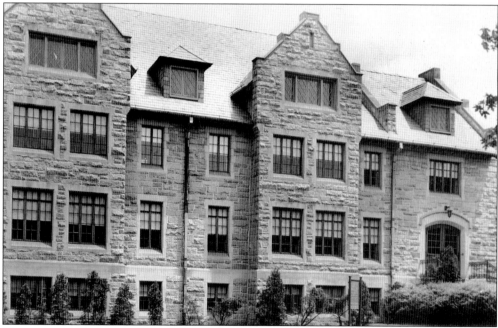

CATONSVILLE UNITED METHODIST CHURCH, C. 1938. In 1925, the church purchased land from the Catonsville Water Company and erected a Sunday school and community center. The Gothic Revival structure was designed by Walker M. Geiske. The new church, proposed by Geiske, was never erected, and the community center eventually housed the church as well. The 1887 church and parsonage were razed. (Courtesy of the Enoch Pratt Free Library.)

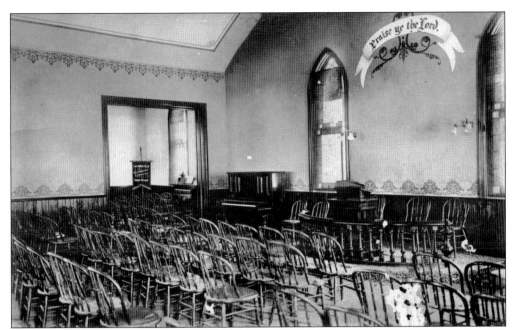

CATONSVILLE UNITED METHODIST CHURCH SUNDAY SCHOOL, C. 1908. The banner in the alcove to the left reads, "Catonsville Methodist Episcopal Sunday School." Note the elegant stencil work at chair rail level and the ceiling line. (Courtesy of William Hollifield.)

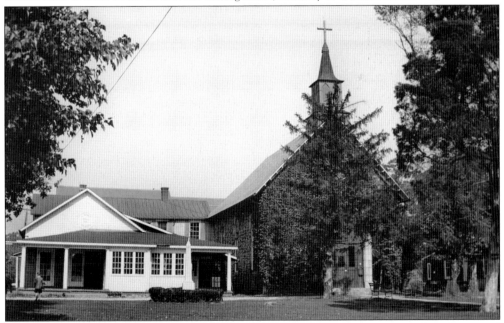

ST. AGNES CATHOLIC CHURCH, BUILT 1853. A Mrs. Sommerville was a major benefactor and was given the honor of naming the church. She selected St. Agnes, after her daughter. When St. Mark Church was built in 1889, to be centrally located to Catonsville residents, St. Agnes was given the status of mission. It regained its status as a church in 1922, and the convent and a new school (currently in danger of being razed) were added. A larger church was later erected. (Courtesy of the Enoch Pratt Free Library.)

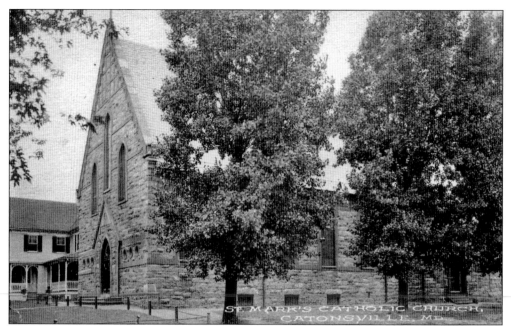

ST. MARK CATHOLIC CHURCH, C. 1920—BUILT IN 1889. An altar of Italian marble was added in 1893, and frescoes were painted in 1905 by Louis Costaggini, son of the late Filippo Costaggini, who painted the frescoes in the Baltimore Cathedral. Pictured here is the church before the vestibule was added in 1925. The old parsonage can be seen to the left. The church has been known as the chapel since the construction of the larger church in 1950. (Courtesy of the Catonsville Room.)

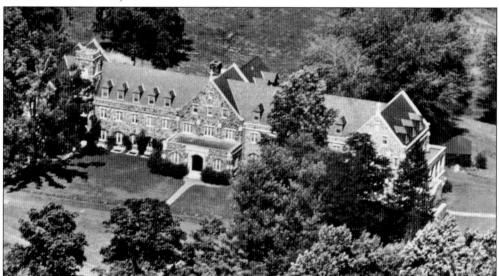

ALL SAINTS SISTERS OF THE POOR CONVENT AND CHAPEL. In 1917, the All Saints Sisters of the Poor community moved to the Country Home for Children, built by the Fresh Air Fund in 1910 at the end of Hilton Avenue. The area is also known as "Orange Grove," named after the flourmill that operated on the nearby Patapsco River. Today the sisters have gained worldwide recognition for the artistic greeting cards they produce to help support themselves. (Courtesy of William Hollifield.)

Six

SANITARIUMS

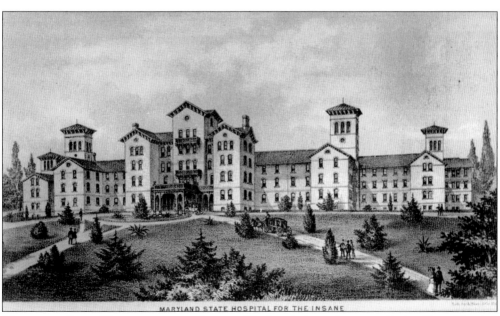

MARYLAND STATE HOSPITAL FOR THE INSANE. The hospital, now known as Spring Grove Hospital Center, was founded in 1797 by Jeremiah Yellott, who established what was called "a Retreat" for ailing mariners in Baltimore. By 1852, it was decided that the hospital needed to relocate to a less urban, more pastoral setting that could accommodate 200 to 250 beds. A 136-acre parcel of land was quickly purchased in Catonsville, and construction began in 1853. This lithograph is by Holm & Company, 1882. (Courtesy of the Enoch Pratt Free Library.)

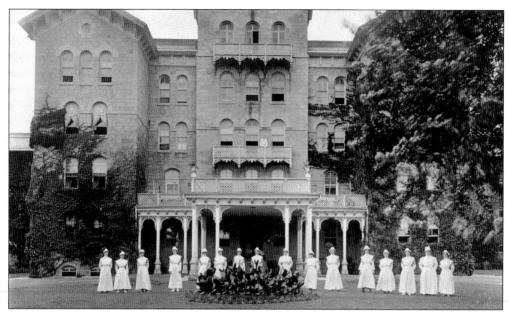

SPRING GROVE NURSES IN FRONT OF THE "OLD MAIN" BUILDING, C. 1890. Progress was slow in the building of the new hospital and halted during the Civil War. The nearly complete Old Main section served as an army hospital for Union soldiers. After the war, construction was completed. On October 7, 1872, the hospital officially relocated, transferring 112 patients to its new location at Spring Grove. The Old Main building was demolished in 1964. All that remains of the original complex is the boiler house. (Courtesy of the Catonsville Room.)

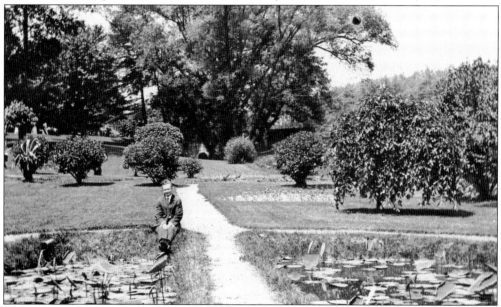

SPRING GROVE LILY PONDS. Dr. Richard F. Gundry Sr. was the medical superintendent from 1878 to 1891. He discontinued the use of all mechanical restraints, a first for psychiatric facilities. Dr. Gundry was responsible for the beautification of the institution's grounds. Many springs on the estate formed a number of ponds surrounding the buildings. The lily pond shown here was in the southeast area of the hospital grounds. (Courtesy of the Catonsville Room.)

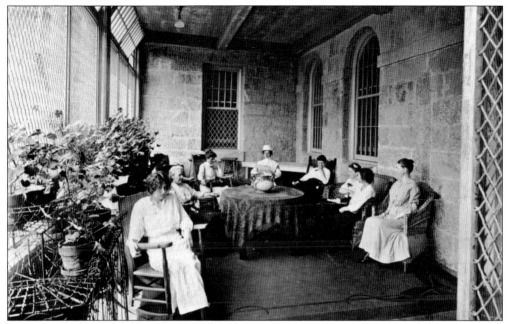

SPRING GROVE SUN PORCH, C. 1915. The porch was located in the south wing of the Old Main building, which was designated for female patients. Note the bars on the windows and fencing surrounding the porch. (Courtesy of the Catonsville Room.)

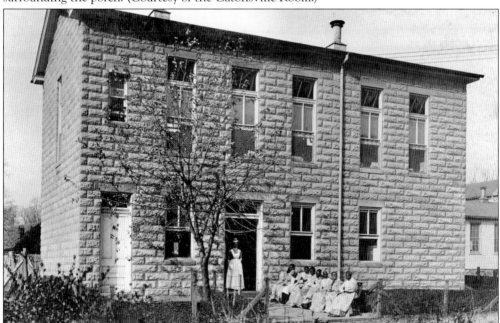

SPRING GROVE COTTAGE FOR COLORED WOMEN, C. 1906. African American patients were admitted to Spring Grove well before the Civil War, at a time when Maryland was still a slave state. It was the first hospital building built specifically for African American psychiatric patients in the state of Maryland. The Hospital for the Negro Insane of Maryland, now Crownsville Hospital Center, was not founded until 1910. In 1913, it became the "TB Cottage" for white, female patients that suffered from tuberculosis. (Courtesy of the Catonsville Room.)

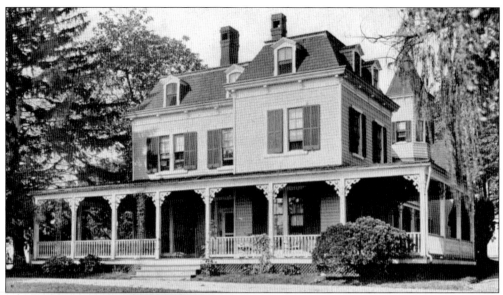

PINE CREST SANITARIUM, C. 1910. The home, located on 20 acres, was originally built in 1865 as a summer retreat known as Mount Brandon. In 1900, it was purchased by Anna A. Sieling, R.N. (1867–1951), an emigrant of Prussia, for the establishment of a private sanitarium she named Pine Crest. An advertisement for the sanitarium states this was "a well equipped sanitarium for the treatment of mental, nervous diseases and drug and alcohol habits, etc." (Courtesy of Scott Trapnell Hilleary.)

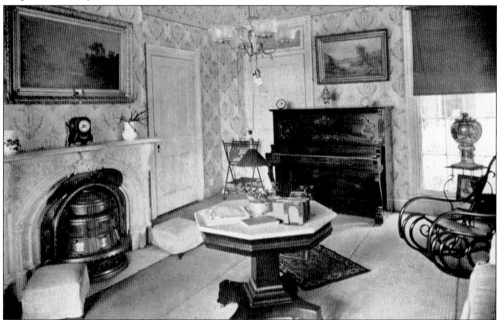

PINE CREST SANITARIUM DRAWING ROOM, C. 1910. In 1939, Miss Sieling turned the sanitarium over to her nephew Hammond P. Dorsey, Esq., for whom she had earlier built Hammond Hall (see page 59) on an acre of the Pine Crest property. The home was built at the furthermost edge of the property so that Dorsey would not be "bothered by the noises and smells of the sanitarium." (Courtesy of Scott Trapnell Hilleary.)

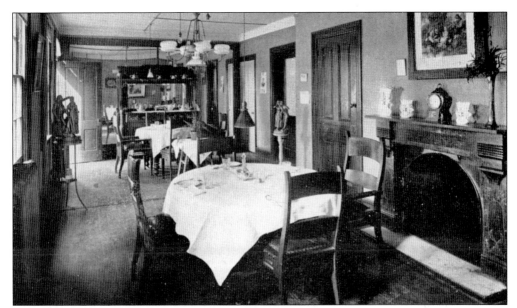

PINE CREST SANITARIUM DINING ROOM, C. 1910. "The Sanitarium is located about one mile west of the Baltimore City limits. The building is large and commodious, of pleasing architecture and is well lighted, both naturally and artificially. The rooms are ample and airy and provided with all necessary comforts and conveniences." Pine Crest was closed in the fall of 1963, and the few remaining patients were transferred to the adjacent property, Ventnor Lodge (see page 58). (Courtesy of Scott Trapnell Hilleary.)

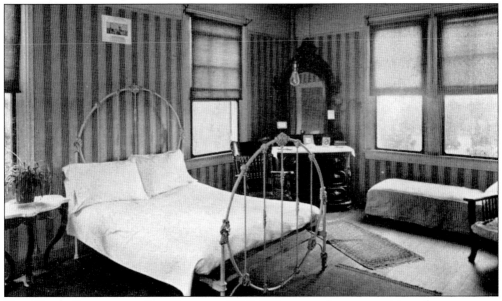

PINE CREST SANITARIUM BED ROOM, C. 1910. "The grounds, compromising of twenty acres, are quite elevated and afforded a splendid view of the surrounding country, with glimpses of the City and the Bay. They are well shaded with ornamental and forest trees." In 1967, the former sanitarium was set on fire by vandals and perished. In 1994, the land was preserved in perpetuity by the Maryland Environmental Trust and is the largest undeveloped plot of land in Baltimore City. (Courtesy of Scott Trapnell Hilleary.)

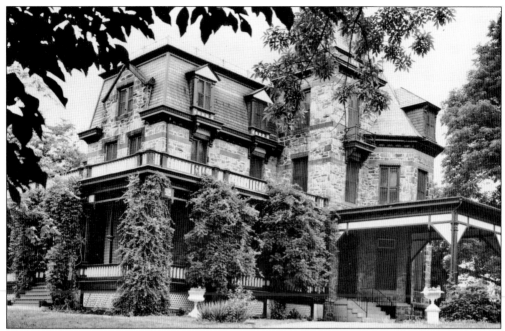

GUNDRY SANITARIUM—2 NORTH WICKHAM ROAD. The house, originally named Athol, was built by Charles Baker in 1880. In 1900, Dr. Alfred Gundry purchased the house and opened a private sanitarium "for the care of nervous disorders of women that require treatment and rest away from home." It continued to function as a sanitarium until 2000. Currently, the house and its outbuildings are in jeopardy of being razed to make room for the new Uplands Development. (Courtesy of the Catonsville Room.)

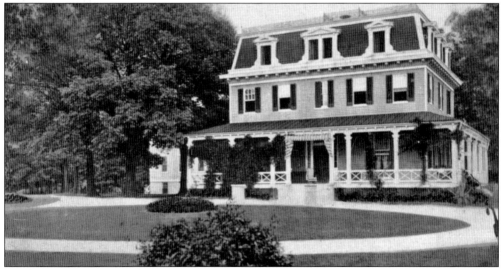

THE RICHARD GUNDY HOUSE, HARLEM LODGE, 327 HARLEM LANE. Dr. Richard Gundy Jr., in 1891, purchased a former home known as Maple Woods, built in 1831, to be use as a private sanitarium "for the treatment of nervous disorders, selected cases of alcoholic and opium habits, neurasthenia, psychasthenia, and various other forms of mental disease requiring removal from environments of home, an ideal place for recuperation from effects of overwork; situated on one of the highest elevations in Balto. Co." (Courtesy of the author's collection.)

Seven

FACES AND PLACES

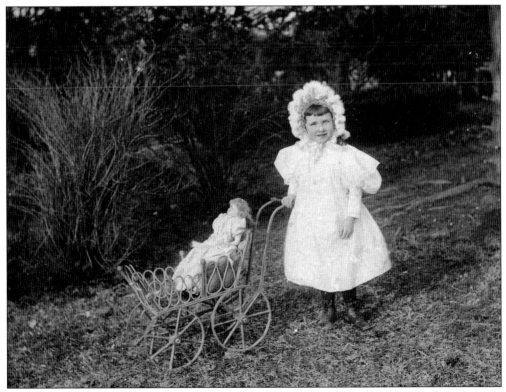

ESSIE STERN, C. 1895. Essie married a man named Smeak and lived at 1407 Chelton Avenue. The home, built in 1880, remains a private residence and the only house in Catonsville with a Chelton Avenue address. (Courtesy of the Catonsville Room.)

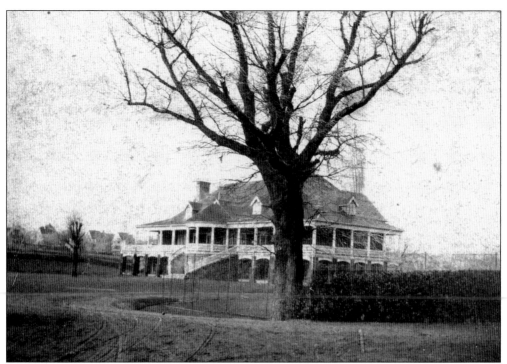

CATONSVILLE COUNTRY CLUB AND CASINO, C. 1891. The club was built in 1891 by wealthy Catonsville residents wanting a "gathering spot," on 18 acres donated by John L. Glenn. It was the first country club built south of New York. It was primarily an athletic club with a bowling alley, nine-hole golf course, and tennis courts. Wilbur and Orville Wright played tennis here, and many New York millionaires gave dances for their daughters who were attending St. Timothy's School. It burned in 1906. (Courtesy of the Catonsville Room.)

-: **BIG DANCE** :-

AT THE

Catonsville Casino

THURS. SEPT. 5th, 1935 from 9 to 2 a. m.

'Mack' CROCKETT'S

Broadcasting Orchestra

Admission :-: 30 Cents

CATONSVILLE CASINO TICKET, 1935. "BIG DANCE at the Catonsville Casino, THURS. SEPT. 5th, 1935 from 9 to 2 a.m. 'Mack' Crockett's Broadcasting Orchestra. Admission 30 cents." (Courtesy of James Vidmar.)

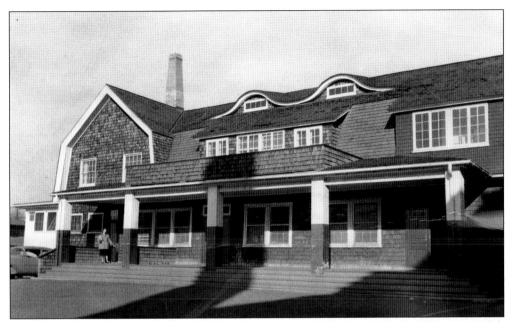

THE NEW CATONSVILLE COUNTRY CLUB. In 1908, a new clubhouse was built. The country club closed for good in 1924. The property was sold to the Baltimore County Board of Education only after a court action, because John Glenn had stipulated that the land only be used for a country club. Catonsville High School used the building as a cafeteria from 1924 to 1925. The building was razed in 1963. (Courtesy of the Catonsville Room.)

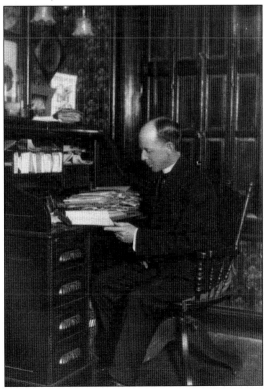

REV. JOHN CULLEN BOWERS (B. 1857). He was the fourth pastor of Salem Lutheran Church and served the congregation for 35 years. He retired in 1947 at the age of 90. (Courtesy of the Catonsville Room.)

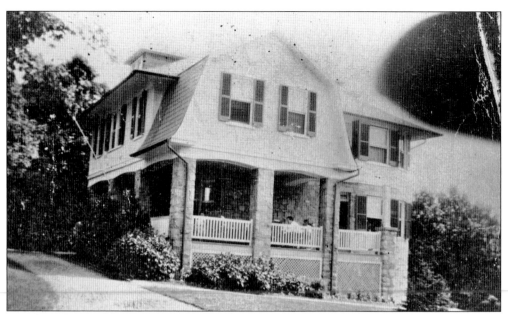

BLOOMSBURY AVENUE, NUMBER 200, 1939. The house, built in 1900, is pictured here when it was the home of Henry and Beulah Brosenne. Their daughter Trudy received notoriety when she became known as "the girl in the iron lung." Since 1975, the house has belonged to the International Society for Krishna Consciousness. (Courtesy of Catherine Anne "Muzzy" Fisher.)

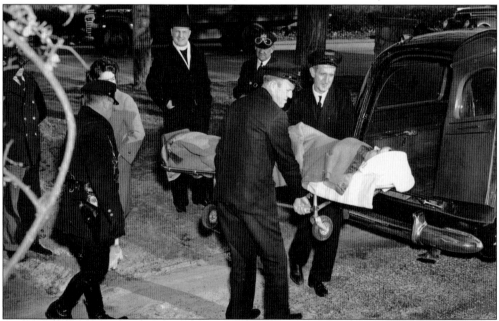

ROSE GERTRUDE "TRUDY" BROSENNE (1927–1953). At the age of 16, Trudy, a student at Catonsville High School, contracted polio. She lived in an iron lung at Sydenham Hospital for Communicable Diseases in Baltimore for 17 months. On January 17, 1946, when she was able to breath on her own, albeit for short periods of time, she was released from the hospital. She came home by ambulance with police escorts, breathing on her own for 36 minutes. (Courtesy of Catherine Anne "Muzzy" Fisher.)

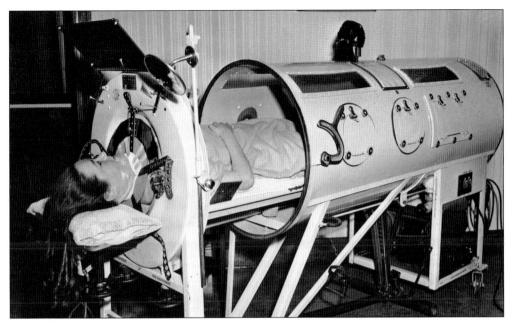

TRUDY BROSENNE IN HER IRON LUNG. Although confined to her iron lung, Trudy did not lead a dull life. When the Ice-capades came to the Fifth Regiment Armory, Trudy was there to see it firsthand. J. Norman Geipe Moving Company transported Trudy, in her iron lung, in a moving van with an electric generator to the ice show, where she had a ringside view. Trudy often wrote, with her teeth, letters to other shut-ins. (Courtesy of Catherine Anne "Muzzy" Fisher.)

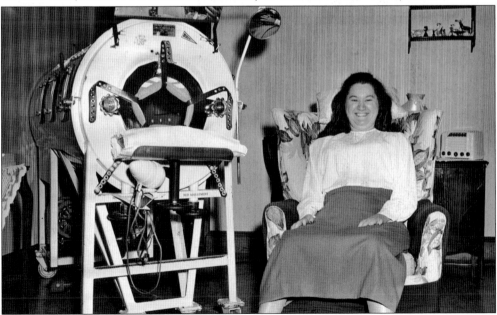

TRUDY BROSENNE. Trudy was eventually able to leave her iron long for a few hours a day. She was a devout Catholic and the only individual allowed to venerate the relic of St. Francis Xavier's right arm outside of a church, requiring special permission from the Pope. On Christmas Day in 1953, Trudy suffered a heart attack and died the next day at the age of 26. (Courtesy of Catherine Anne "Muzzy" Fisher.)

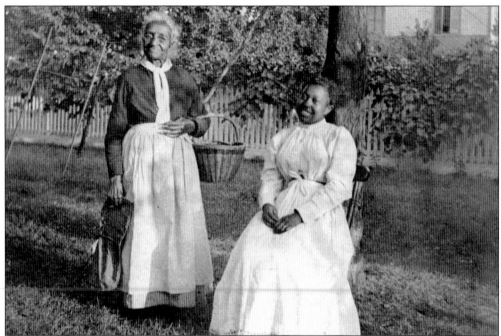

AUNT KITTY SUGARS AND CORNELIA SQUIRREL, C. 1890. Before and after slavery, the Winters Lane area was the home for numerous African Americans. Most emigrated down from Harristown, a small area on the upper end of Winters Lane. Many served as domestics to the families of Catonsville. The women pictured here were servants to the Jones family at 10 Newburg Avenue. (Courtesy of the Catonsville Room.)

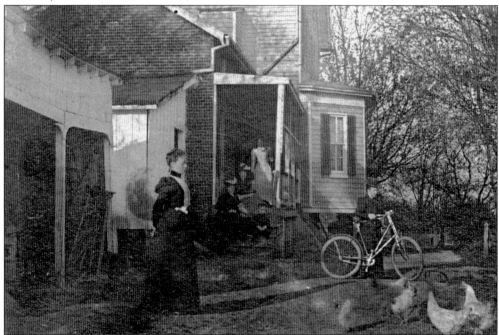

JONES HOUSE, 10 NEWBURG AVENUE. Pictured here are Eda Standing (in the foreground) and Julia Jones (with the bicycle). Others are unidentified. (Courtesy of the Catonsville Room.)

AUNT KITTY SUGARS, C. 1890. Aunt Kitty saw first-hand the end of slavery. (Courtesy of the Catonsville Room.)

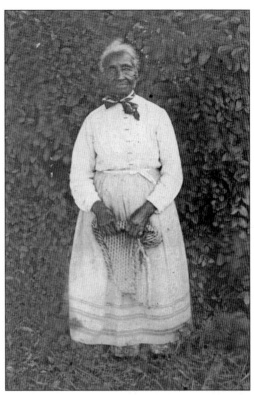

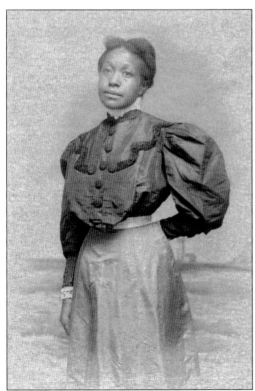

CORNELIA SQUIRREL, C. 1890. Cornelia is photographed here in her Sunday best. (Courtesy of the Catonsville Room.)

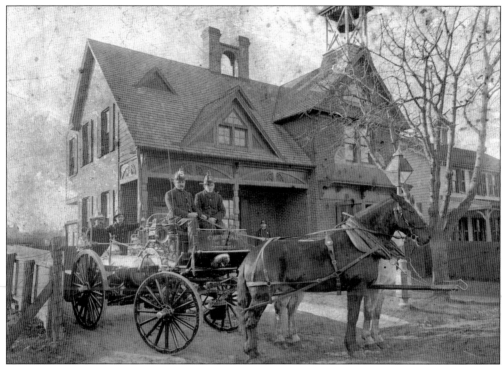

EDWARD A. POEHLMANN DRIVING THE CATONSVILLE CHEMICAL WAGON, C. 1890. The fire station was located at 22 Bloomsbury Avenue from 1889 to 1928. By 1894, the fire station possessed the latest in firefighting equipment. The Holloway's Chemical Engine consisted of two tanks with a capacity of 180 gallons and was pulled by two horses. (Courtesy of Calvin S. Wiley.)

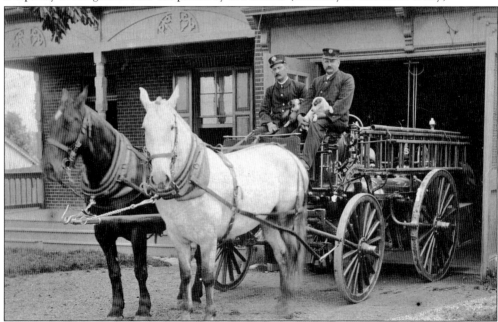

CHEMICAL WAGON, 1905. Pictured from left to right are Tom Armacost, Edward A. Poehlmann, and two unnamed canine companions. (Courtesy of Calvin S. Wiley.)

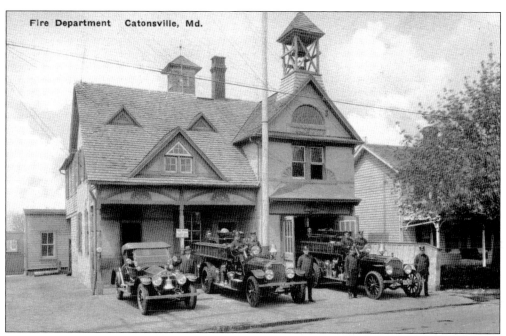

MOTORIZED FIRE TRUCKS. By 1908, Baltimore County's first motorized firefighting vehicles came to Catonsville. This postcard depicts two of the early fire trucks. The fire chief's car is seen on the left. (Courtesy of William Hollifield.)

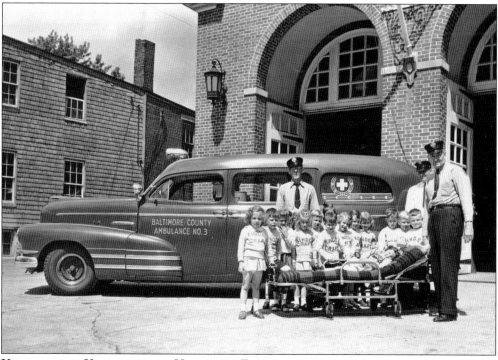

KINDERCRAFT KINDERGARTEN VISITS THE FIREHOUSE, C. 1946. In 1928, a new police-fire complex was built at the corner of Frederick Road and Egges Lane. The Bloomsbury Avenue station house is currently used as an office building. (Courtesy of the Catonsville Room.)

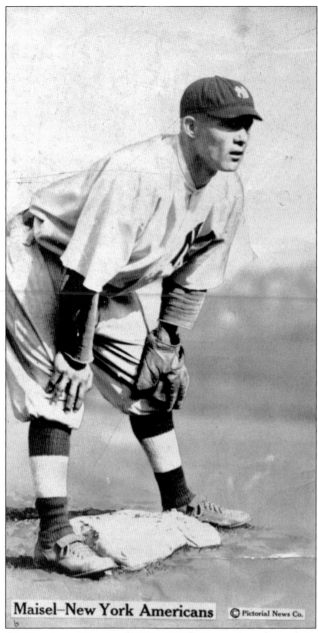

Maisel–New York Americans ©Pictorial News Co.

FREDERICK "FRITZ" CHARLES MAISEL (1889–1967). Sometimes known as "the Flash," Fritz played professional baseball from 1913 to 1918 with the International League Orioles, the New York Yankees, and the St. Louis Browns. Generally a third baseman, he also played second base or in the outfield. While playing third base for the New York Yankees in 1914, he set a record for stolen bases and was considered a fast, brainy, and aggressive star player. His record of 74 stolen bases with the Yankees stood until 1988, when Rickey Henderson finished the season having stolen 93 bases for New York. He was manager of the old Orioles from 1929 to 1932. When he retired from baseball, Maisel returned to Catonsville and joined the Baltimore County Fire Department, and he was chief from 1938 to 1951. His brother George Maisel also played professional baseball off and on from 1913 to 1922. (Courtesy of the Catonsville Room.)

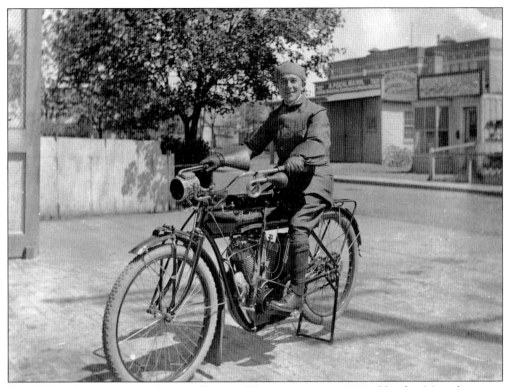

LAWRENCE SEICKE ON AN INDIAN SINGLE MOTORCYCLE, C. 1910. Hendee Manufacturing Company of Springfield, Massachusetts, produced the first "motor driven bicycle" in 1901. The 1901 Indian had a 1.75-horsepower engine that could propel the machine almost as fast as 25 miles per hour. In the background can be seen Poehlmann's Blacksmith Shop and Cairnes Plumbing. (Courtesy of the Catonsville Room.)

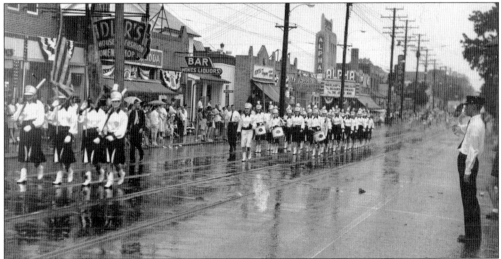

FOURTH OF JULY PARADE, 1956. Catonsville has had a long tradition of celebrating the Fourth of July with parades and fireworks. Jean S. Walsh recalls this particularly rainy Fourth: "My son was in a marching band. That morning I quickly sewed a cover out of plastic with a zipper to protect his drum from the rain." (Courtesy of the Catonsville Room.)

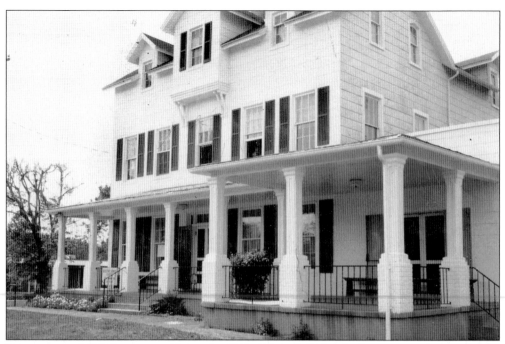

BEAUMONT—1010 FREDERICK ROAD. In 1866, Edwin J. Farber built a country house that he named Beaumont. Farber was a distinguished lawyer in both America and Europe. He was the founder and editor of the *Meteor*, the first newspaper in Catonsville. The paper became the *Argus*, the precursor to today's *Catonsville Times*. In the 1920s, the Knights of Columbus made it their lodge. The building had a decorative trim that is now covered by the aluminum siding. (Courtesy of the Catonsville Room.)

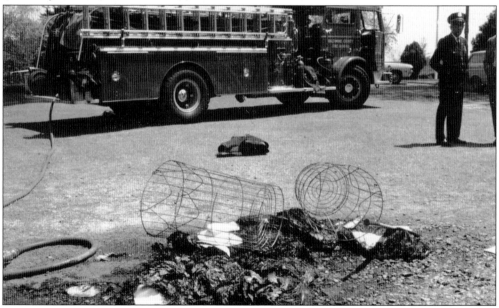

BURNT DRAFT CARD REMAINS, 1968. "Our apologies, good friends, for the fracture of good order, the burning of paper instead of children . . ." This quote is from Daniel Berrigan, leader of the infamous Catonsville Nine. (Courtesy of the Catonsville Room.)

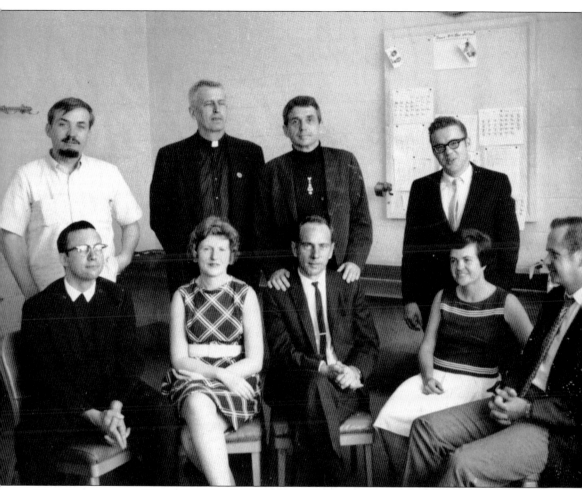

THE CATONSVILLE NINE. On May 17, 1968, nine Vietnam War protesters walked into the Selective Service office, located on the second floor of the Knights of Columbus Lodge, and removed 378 A-1 draft files. They incinerated the records with homemade napalm in the parking lot. Pictured from left to right are as follows: (first row) Thomas Melvin, Marjorie Melvin, John Hogan, Mary Moylan, and George Mische; (second row) Thomas Lewis, Rev. Philip Berrigan, Rev. Daniel Berrigan, and David Darst. The photograph was taken by Jean S. Walsh when the nine were being held at the Wilkins Avenue police station. When asked if they minded having their photograph taken, the group quickly pushed chairs together and posed. All nine were charged with sabotage, robbery, and assault. They were all convicted and served jail time. In 1970, Daniel Berrigan, no longer a Catholic priest and still imprisoned, wrote a play from the trial transcripts. *The Trial of the Catonsville Nine* movie was produced in 1972 by actor Gregory Peck. (Courtesy of the Catonsville Room.)

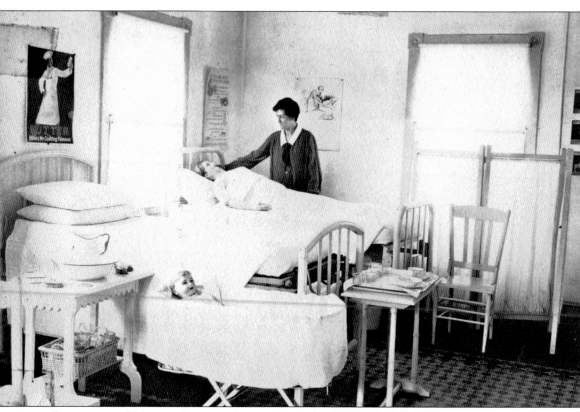

Catonsville Health Center, April 1930. The first public health center in Catonsville was opened in 1926 and located at 19 Egges Lane. Miss L. Hiss was the first public health nurse assigned to the center. She is seen in this photograph demonstrating home nursing techniques. Notice that her patients are dolls. (Courtesy of the Catonsville Room.)